KARMIC RELATIONSHIPS VOL. IV

D1527618

KARMIC RELATIONSHIPS

Esoteric Studies

Vol. IV

RUDOLF STEINER

*Eleven lectures given at Dornach,
Switzerland, between 5th and 24th
September, 1924*

Translated by George Adams,
D. S. Osmond and C. Davey

RUDOLF STEINER PRESS

Rudolf Steiner Press
Hillside House, The Square
Forest House RH18 5ES

www.rudolfsteinerpress.com

First edition 1957
Second edition 1965
Reprinted 1997, with the addition of 'The Last Address', 2008
Reprinted in paperback 2017

Originally published in German under the title *Esoterische Betrachtungen
karmischer Zusammenhänge, Vierter Band: Das geistige Leben der
Gegenwart im Zusammenhang mit der anthroposophischen Bewegung*
(volume 238 in the *Rudolf Steiner Gesamtausgabe* or Collected Works) by
Rudolf Steiner Verlag, Dornach. This authorized translation published
by kind permission of the Rudolf Steiner Nachlassverwaltung, Dornach

A catalogue record for this book is available from the British Library

ISBN 978 1 85584 538 1

Printed and bound in Great Britain by 4Edge Ltd., Essex

SUMMARY OF CONTENTS

into spirituality the intellectualism of the present age is the task of Anthroposophy, which must reckon with the rationalism of the times in order that man may find the path of ideas upward to the Spirit no less than downward into nature. At the end of the 19th century the spiritual element in human souls was dammed up, and in order to reveal itself in any way had to draw back from intellectualism. It will be evident in such men how they shrink from being touched too deeply by modern intellectualism. Plato and the individuality reborn as Goethe.

Dornach, 23rd September, 1924

11

Dornach, 28th September, 1924

EDITOR'S PREFACE

During the year 1924, before his illness in September, Rudolf Steiner gave over eighty lectures, published with the title *Karmic Relationships: Esoteric Studies*, to members of the Anthroposophical Society in the following places: Dornach, Berne, Zürich, Stuttgart, Prague, Paris, Breslau, Arnhem, Torquay and London. English translations of these lectures are contained in the following volumes of the series:

Vols. I to IV. Lectures given in Dornach (49).
Vol. V. Lectures given in Prague (4) and Paris (3).
Vol. VI. Lectures given in Berne (2) Zürich (1), Stuttgart (3) Arnhem (3).
Vol. VII. Lectures given in Breslau (9).
Vol. VIII. Lectures given in Torquay (3) and London (3).

All these lectures were given to members of the Anthroposophical Society only and were intended to be material for study by those already familiar with the fundamental principles of Anthroposophy. The following extract from the lecture of 22nd June, 1924 (see Vol. II) calls attention to the need for exactitude when passing on such contents:

"The study of problems connected with karma is by no means easy and the discussion of anything that has to do with the subject entails—or ought at any rate to entail—a sense of deep responsibility. Such study is in truth a matter of penetrating into the most profound mysteries of existence, for within the sphere of karma and the course it takes lie those processes which are the basis of the other phenomena of world-existence, even of the phenomena of nature.... These difficult and weighty matters entail grave consideration of every word and every sentence spoken here, in order that *the limits within which the statements are made shall be absolutely clear....*"

The attention of readers is called to the fact that the fundamental explanations given by Rudolf Steiner of the laws and conditions of karma are contained in Vol. I of the series. Knowledge of the earlier lectures should therefore be regarded as an essential basis for study of those contained in the later volumes.

Lecture 1

INTRODUCTION

Many friends have come here to-day for the first time since the Christmas Foundation Meeting and I must therefore speak of it, even if only briefly, by way of introduction. Through this Christmas Foundation the Anthroposophical Society was to be given a new impulse, the impulse that is essential if it is to be a worthy channel for the life which, through Anthroposophy, must find embodiment in human civilisation. Since the Christmas Foundation an esoteric impulse has indeed come into the Anthroposophical Society. Hitherto this society was as it were the administrative centre for Anthroposophy. From its beginning onwards, Anthroposophy was the channel for the spiritual life that has been accessible to mankind since the last third of the 19th century. Our conception of the Anthroposophical Movement, however, must be that what takes its course on earth is only the outer manifestation of something that is accomplished in the spiritual world for the furtherance of the evolution of humanity. And those who wish to be worthily connected with the Anthroposophical Movement must also realise that the spiritual impulses are also at work in the sphere of the Anthroposophical Society itself.

What does it really amount to when a man has a general, theoretical belief in a spiritual world ? To believe in theory in a spiritual world means to receive it into one's thoughts. But although in their own original nature thoughts represent the most spiritual element in modern man, the thoughts themselves are such that in their development as inner spirit during the last four to five centuries, they are adapted only to receive truths relating to material existence. And so people to-day have a spiritual life in thoughts, but as members of contemporary civilisation they fill it with a material content only. Theoretical knowledge of Anthroposophy also remains a material content until there is added to it the inner, conscious power of conviction that the spiritual is concrete reality; that wherever matter exists for the outer eyes of men, not only does spirit permeate this matter, but everything material finally vanishes before man's true perception, when this is able to penetrate through the material to the spiritual.

But such perception must then extend also to everything that is our own close concern. Our membership of the Anthroposophical Society is such a concern; it is a fact in the outer world. And we must be able to recognise the spiritual reality corresponding to it, the spiritual movement which in the modern age unfolded in the spiritual world and will go forward in earthly life if men do but keep faith with it. Otherwise it will go forward apart from earthly life; its link with earthly life will be maintained if men find in their hearts the strength to keep faith with it.

It is not enough to acknowledge theoretically that spiritual reality hovers behind mineral, plant, animal and man himself; what must penetrate as deep conviction into the heart of every professed Anthroposophist is that behind the Anthroposophical Society too—which in its outward aspect belongs to the world of maya, of illusion—there hovers the spiritual archetype of the Anthroposophical Movement. This conviction must take real effect in the work and activity of the Anthroposophical Society. Before the Christmas Foundation Meeting I often said that a distinction must be made between the Anthroposophical Movement and the Anthroposophical Society, which was an exoteric administrative centre for anthroposophical esotericism. Since Christmas, the opposite holds good. In all previous years I considered myself to be the teacher of Anthroposophy apart altogether from the affairs of administration, and I adhered strictly to this principle. The Anthroposophical Society as such was directed by others. What devolved upon me was to present Anthroposophy to the Groups who wished for this.

12

In the course of the lectures now being given, or in some other way, friends will be able to understand what it means to present on the earthly plane what is revealed in the spiritual world to-day; and the difficulties that arise when external administrative requirements are added to this connection with the spiritual world should be realised. At Christmas there was this eventuality: either the Spiritual Powers who endow us with Anthroposophy would take exception to the outer administrative business being connected in some way with esotericism itself, or something different would result. Hence the decision that had then to be taken was an extremely difficult one. For it might well have happened that the stream of spiritual life that has been vouchsafed to us would have been endangered as a result.

Nevertheless, the decision was essential if Anthroposophy was to remain connected with the Anthroposophical Society. In future the Anthroposophical Society itself must be the centre through which the esoteric life flows, and must be conscious of it.

The esoteric Vorstand had then to be created at the Goetheanum. It was necessary to recognise that an esoteric task devolves upon this Vorstand as a whole and that in the future everything that flows through the Anthroposophical Society must not only be material to be assimilated but that Anthroposophy, as well as being a teaching, must be put into effect in all external measures.

It was necessary that there should be recognition of those forces which must unite the individual personalities in the Society. Such forces cannot be the subject of any programme or abstractly formulated statements. Human relationships in the truly esoteric sense can provide the only foundation for the Anthroposophical Society. In the future, therefore, everything must be based upon real human relationships in the widest sense, upon concrete, not abstract, spiritual life.

It is a matter of grasping the reality of the spiritual life as such and putting it into practice in every detail of existence. Let me speak of one small matter. We decided to issue a new membership card to each of our members, of whom there are now twelve thousand. It was therefore a matter of preparing this number of membership cards, and in spite of an objection made by several people, I was obliged to decide to sign each card myself. This was naturally a task that took several weeks. But what does it mean? It means that my eyes have rested upon the name of the one who receives the card of membership. This is not the outcome of anything like arrogance, nor is it a purely administrative matter. It is the expression of a human relationship, perhaps a seemingly unimportant one at first, but for all that it is a human relationship.

In this way, human relationships—which are facts—differ from administrative regulations and statements contained in programmes and paragraphs. The content of Anthroposophy cannot be formulated in sentences and clauses but must be life, real life, which alone can assimilate esotericism.

And so it must be emphasised that since the Christmas Foundation, Anthroposophy and the Anthroposophical Society are no longer to be distinguished from each other, for they have become one. What matters above all is that every single member shall be conscious of this. It may seem to you that this is a natural matter of course, but if you think about it you will find that it is by no means an easy matter; it is actually extremely difficult to act in accordance with it every minute of one's life.

Anxiety is inevitable as to whether, under these conditions, spiritual life will continue to flow through the Anthroposophical Society as it did through the Anthroposophical Movement. However, now that we have been living for many months under the influence of the Christmas Foundation, endeavouring to be true to what was intended in the laying of the spiritual Foundation Stone of the Anthroposophical Society, we may justifiably say to ourselves that what has been flowing to us for years is flowing in even greater abundance. It may also be said that hearts have been even more receptive wherever the more

14

esoteric trend, which since the Christmas Foundation, has pervaded all anthroposophical work. Take the whole significance of what I have said as the result of the experiences of recent months, into your hearts, my dear friends. Such a conception will in the future contribute in many ways to the provision of the right soil for that spiritual Foundation Stone which was laid for the Anthroposophical Society at the time of the Christmas Meeting.

And this brings me to speak of what I shall have to say to you in the coming days, for which this introductory lecture is intended to provide guiding lines. I want to show how at this serious point in its existence the Anthroposophical Movement is actually returning to its own germinal impulse. When at the beginning of the century the Anthroposophical Society came into being out of the framework of the Theosophical Society, something very characteristic was foreshadowed. While the Anthroposophical Society—then the German Section of the Theosophical Society—was in process of formation, I gave lectures in Berlin on *Anthroposophy*. Therewith, at the very outset, my work was given the hallmark of the impulse which later became an integral part of the Anthroposophical Movement.

Apart from this, I can remind you to-day of something else.—The first few lectures I was to give at that time to a very small circle were to have the title, " Practical Exercises for the Understanding of Karma." I became aware of intense opposition to this proposal. And perhaps Herr Guenther Wagner, now the oldest member of the Anthroposophical Society, who to our great joy is here to-day and whom I want to welcome most cordially as an Elder of the society, will remember how strong was the opposition at that time to much that from the beginning onwards I was to incorporate in the Anthroposophical Movement.

Those lectures were not given. In face of the other currents emanating from the Theosophical Movement it was not possible to proceed with the cultivation of the esotericism which speaks unreservedly of the reality of what was always there in the form of theory.

15

Since the Christmas Foundation, the concrete working of karma in historical happenings and in individual human beings has been spoken of without reserve in this hall* and in the various places I have been able to visit. And a number of Anthroposophists have already heard how the different earthly lives of significant personalities have run their course, how the karma of the Anthroposophical Society itself and of the individuals connected with it has taken shape. Since the Christmas Foundation these things have been spoken of in a fully esoteric sense; but since the Christmas Foundation, also, our printed Lecture-Courses have been accessible to everyone interested in them. We have thus become an esoteric and at the same time a completely open society.

Thus we return in a certain sense to the starting-point. What must now be reality was then intention. As many friends are here for the first time since the Christmas Foundation, I shall be speaking to you in the coming lectures on questions of karma, giving a kind of introduction to-day by speaking of things which are also indicated, briefly, in the current News Sheet for members of the society.

As is clear from our anthroposophical literature, the development of human consciousness is bound up with the attainment of those data of knowledge which point to facts and beings of the spiritual world and with penetration into these facts. We shall hear how this spiritual world, the penetration into which has become possible through the development of human consciousness, can then be intelligible to the healthy, unprejudiced human intellect. It must always be remembered that although actual penetration into the spiritual world requires the development of other states of consciousness, the understanding of what the spiritual investigator brings to light requires only the healthy human intellect, the healthy human reason that endeavours to put prejudice aside.

In saying this, one immediately meets stubborn obstacles in the modern life of thought. When I once said the same

* The temporary lecture-hall in the " Schreinerei " (workshop) at the Goetheanum.

16

thing in Berlin, a well-meaning article appeared on the subject of the public lecture I had given before a large audience. This article was to the following effect: Steiner maintains that the healthy human intellect can understand what is investigated in the spiritual world. But the whole trend of modern times has taught us that the healthy human intellect can know nothing of the supersensible world, and that if it does, it is certainly not healthy!

It must be admitted that in a certain sense this is the general opinion of cultured people at the present time. What it means, translated into bald language, is this: If a man is not mad, he understands nothing of the supersensible world; if he does, then he is certainly mad! That is the same way of speaking about the subject, only put rather more plainly.

We must try to comprehend, therefore, how far the healthy human intellect can gain insight into the results of spiritual investigation achieved through the development of states of consciousness other than those we are familiar with in ordinary life. For centuries now we have been arming our senses with laboratory apparatus, with telescopes, microscopes and the like. The spiritual investigator arms his outer senses with what he himself develops in his own soul. Investigation of nature has gone outwards, has made use of outer instruments. Spiritual investigation goes inwards, makes use of the inner instruments evolved by the soul in steadfast activity of the inner life.

By way of introduction to-day I want to help you to understand the evolution of other states of consciousness, first of all simply by comparing those that are normal in present-day man with those that were once present in earlier, primitive—not historic but prehistoric—conditions of human evolution.

Man lives to-day in three states of consciousness, only one of which, really, he recognises as a source of knowledge. They are:

Ordinary waking consciousness;
Dream consciousness;
Dreamless sleep consciousness.

In ordinary waking consciousness we confront the outer world in such a way that we accept as reality what can be grasped through the senses, and allow it to work upon us; we grasp this outer, material world with the intellect that is bound to the brain, or at any rate to the human organism, and we form ideas, concepts, emotions and feelings, too, about what has been taken in through the senses. Then in this waking consciousness we grasp the reality of our own inner life—within certain limits. And through all kinds of reflection, through the development of ideas, we come to acknowledge the existence of a supersensible element above material things. I need not further describe this state of consciousness; it is known to everyone as the state he recognises as pertaining to his life of knowledge and of will here on earth.

For the man of the present time, dream consciousness is indistinct and dim. In dream consciousness he sees things of the outer world in symbolic transformations which he does not always recognise as such. A man lying in bed in the morning, still in the process of waking, does not look out at the rising sun with fully opened eyes; to his still veiled gaze the sunlight reveals itself by shining in through the window. He is still separated as by a thin veil from what at other times he grasps in sharply outlined sense-experiences and perceptions. Inwardly, his soul is filled with the picture of a great fire; the heat of the fire in his dream symbolises the shining in of the rising sun upon eyes not yet fully opened.

Or again, someone may dream that he is passing through lines of white stones placed along each side of a roadway. He comes to one of the stones and finds that it has been demolished by some force of nature or by the hand of man. He wakes up; the toothache he feels makes him aware of the decayed state of a tooth. The two rows of teeth have been symbolised in his dream-picture; the decayed tooth, in the image of the demolished stone.

Or we become aware of being, apparently, in an overheated room where we feel discomfort. We wake up: the heart is thumping vigorously and the pulse beating rapidly. The feverish movement of the heart and pulse is symbolised in the overheated room. Inner and outer conditions are symbolised in dream; reminiscences of the life of day, transformed and elaborated in manifold ways into whole dream-dramas, absorb the sleeper's attention. Nor does he by any means always know to what extent things are elaborated in the miraculous arena of his life of soul. And concerning this dream-life, which may play over into waking life when consciousness is dimmed in any way, he often labours under slight illusions.

A scientist is passing a bookshop in a street. He sees a book about the lower animal species—a book which in view of his profession has always greatly interested him. But now, although the title indicates a content of vital importance to a scientist, he feels not the faintest interest: and then, suddenly, as he is merely staring at what otherwise he would have seen with keen excitement, he hears a barrel-organ in the distance playing a melody which at first entirely escapes his memory . . . and he becomes all attention.—Just think of it: the man is looking at the title of a scientific treatise; he pays no attention to it but is gripped by the playing of a distant barrel-organ which in other circumstances he would not have listened to for a moment. What is the explanation? Forty years ago, while still quite young, he had danced for the first time in his life, with his first partner, to the same tune; he is reminded of this by the tune which he has not heard for forty years, played on the barrel-organ! Because he has remained very matter-of-fact, the scientist remembers the occasion pretty accurately.

The mystic often comes to the stage of inwardly transforming a happening of this kind to such an extent that it becomes something entirely different. One who with deep and sincere conscientiousness embarks upon the task of penetrating into the spiritual life must also keep strictly in mind all the deception and illusion that may arise in the life of the soul. In deepening his life of soul a man can very easily believe that an inner path has been discovered to some spiritual reality, whereas in fact it is no more than the trans-

19

formed reminiscence of a barrel-organ melody! This dream-life is full of wonder and splendour, but can be rightly understood only by one who is able to bring spiritual insight to bear upon the appearances of human life.

Of the life of deep, dreamless sleep, man has in his ordinary consciousness nothing more than the remembrance that time continues to flow between the moment of falling asleep and the moment of waking. Everything else he has to experience again with the help of his waking consciousness. A dim, general feeling of having been present between the moments of falling asleep and waking is all that remains from dreamless sleep.

Thus we have to-day these three states of consciousness: waking consciousness, dream consciousness, dreamless sleep consciousness. If we go back into very early ages of human evolution—not, as I said, in historic times but prehistoric times accessible only to those means of spiritual investigation of which we shall be speaking here in the coming days—then we also find three states of consciousness, but essentially different in character. What we experience to-day in our waking hours was not experienced by the men of those primeval times; instead of material objects and beings with clear shapes and sharp edges, they saw all the physical boundaries blurred.

In those times a man who might have looked at you all sitting here would not have seen the sharp outlines demarcating you as human beings to-day; he would not, like a man to-day, have seen these contours bound by so many lines, but for his ordinary waking consciousness the forms would have been blurred; they would have lacked definition. Everything would have been seen with less precision, would have been pervaded by an aura, by a spiritual radiance, a glimmering, glistening iridescence extending far beyond the circumference that is perceived to-day. The onlooker would have seen how the auras of all of you sitting here are interwoven. He would have gazed into these glimmering, sparkling, iridescent auras of the soul-life of those in front of him. It was still possible in those days to gaze into the life of soul because the human being was bathed in an atmosphere of soul-and-spirit.

To use an analogy: if in the evening of a bright, dry day we are walking through the streets, we see the lights of the street-lamps in definite outlines. But if the evening is misty, we see these same lights haloed by all sorts of colours—colours which modern physics interprets quite wrongly, regarding them as subjective phenomena, whereas in truth they give us an experience of the inmost nature of these lights, connected with the fact that we are moving through the watery element of the fog. The men of ancient times moved through the element of soul-and-spirit; when they looked at other men they saw their auras—which were not subjective phenomena but a real and objective part of the human being. Such was one state of consciousness in these men of old.

Then they had a state of consciousness which linked on to this, just as with us the sleep that is invaded by dreams links on to the waking state; again it was not the same as our present dream condition, but everything that was material around it disappeared, vanished away. For us, sense-impressions become symbols in the state of dream consciousness: sunshine becomes fiery heat, the rows of teeth become two lines of stones, dream-memories become earthly or also spiritual dramas. The sense-world is always there; the world of memories remains. It was different for the consciousness of one who lived in primeval times of human evolution—and we shall realise by and by that this applies to all of us, for those sitting here were present then in earlier earthly lives. In those times, when the sun's light by day grew weaker, man did not see symbols of physical things, but the physical things vanished before his eyes. A tree standing before him vanished; it was transformed into the spiritual and the spirit-being belonging to the tree took its place.—The legends of tree-spirits were not the inventions of folk-fantasy; the interpretation of these legends, however, is an invention of the fantasy of scholars who are groping in a morass of fallacy.—And it was these spirits—the tree-spirit, the mountain-spirit, the spirit of the rocks—who in turn directed the eyes

21

of the human soul into that world where man is between death and a new birth, where he is among spiritual realities just as here on earth he is among physical realities, where he is among spiritual beings as on earth he is among physical beings.—This was the second state of consciousness. We shall presently see how our ordinary dream consciousness can also be transformed into this other consciousness in a man of modern time who is a seeker for spiritual knowledge.

And there was a third state of consciousness. Naturally, the men of ancient times also slept; but when they awoke they had not merely a dim remembrance of having lived through time, or a dim feeling of continuous life, but a clear remembrance of what they had experienced in sleep. And it was precisely out of this sleep that there came the impressions of past earthly lives with their connections of destiny, together with the knowledge, the vision, of *karma*.

Modern man has waking consciousness, dream consciousness, dreamless sleep consciousness. Early humanity had also three states or conditions of consciousness: the state of consciousness in which he perceived reality pervaded by spirit; the state in which he had insight into the spiritual world; and the state in which he had the vision of karma. In primeval humanity, consciousness was essentially in a condition of evening twilight.

This evening twilight consciousness has passed away, has died out in the course of the evolution of mankind. A morning dawn consciousness must arise—into which modern spiritual investigation has already found its way. And by strengthening his own soul-forces man must learn to look at every tree or rock, every spring or mountain, or at the stars, in such a way that the spiritual fact or spiritual being behind every physical thing is revealed to him.

It can become an exact science, a source of exact knowledge (although people scoff at it to-day as if it were craziness or sheer delusion) so that when a genuine knower looks at a tree, the tree, although it represents a physical reality, becomes a void, as it were leaving the space free before his gaze, and the spirit-being of the tree comes to meet him. Just as the sun's light is reflected to our physical eyes from all outer, physical objects, so will humanity come to perceive that the spiritual essence of the sun, pervading the world with its life, is also a living reality in all physical beings. As the physical light is reflected back to our physical eyes, so from every earthly being there can be reflected back as a reality to our eyes of soul, the divine-spiritual, all-pervading essence of the sun. And as man now says: "The rose is red " . . . the underlying truth being that the rose is giving back to him the gift he himself receives from the physical-etheric sun-nature . . . he will then be able to say that the rose gives back to him what it receives from the soul-and-spiritual essence of the sun which streams through the world with its quickening life.

Man will again find his way into a spiritual atmosphere, will know that his own being is rooted in this spiritual atmosphere. He will come to realise that within the dream consciousness, which to begin with can yield only chaotic symbolisations of the outer life of the senses, there lie the revelations of a world of spirit through which we pass between death and a new birth; furthermore, that in the consciousness of deep sleep there weaves and lives in us as an actual and real nexus of forces that which, after waking, leads us into connection with the working out of our destiny, of our karma. What we live through in our waking hours as destiny, notwithstanding all freedom, is spun during our life of sleep, when with the soul and spirit, which have left the physical and etheric, we lead a life together with divine Spirits; with those divine Spirits, too, who carry over the fruits of earlier lives into this present life. And one who through the development of th . corresponding forces of soul succeeds in penetrating with vision into the life of dreamless sleep, discovers therein the connections of karma. Moreover it is only in this way that the historical life of humanity acquires meaning, for it is woven out of what men carry over from earlier epochs, through the life between death and re-birth, into new life, into new epochs. When we look at some personality of the present or some other age, we understand him rightly only when we include his past earthly lives.

During the coming days, then, we shall be speaking of that spiritual investigation which, while concerning itself first with personalities in history but then also with everyday life, leads from the present life, or a life in some other age to earlier earthly lives.

Lecture 2

As I have said, theoretical explanations about karma and repeated earthly lives cannot but remain unliving and inadequate, until our thought in this direction really flows into our understanding of the life around us. We must contemplate life itself in the light of karma and repeated earthly lives. But such a contemplation requires the very greatest earnestness, for it may indeed be said that the temptation is very great for man to spin out all manner of ideas about karmic connections and repeated earthly lives. The temptation is great; the source of illusions in this sphere is exceedingly great. And indeed, real investigations in this sphere can be made only by one to whom the spiritual world has in a sense been opened through his own soul-development.

Hence it must also be said that in these matters especially the investigator must rely on those foundations of conviction in his audience which may follow from other things he has brought to light. Indeed we ought not to have any confidence in one who begins without more ado to speak about repeated earthly lives in detail. What is derived from such occult depths as these must be confirmed and supported by the fact that many other things have already been produced which give a real basis for confidence in the spiritual investigator.

Now I think I may say that in the twenty-three to twenty-four years during which we have cultivated Anthroposophy, enough occult material has been gathered to warrant the description at this present time even of these bold researches into karma and repeated earthly lives, for the benefit of those who may have gained true confidence through the other realms of spiritual life which have been unfolded before them in the course of time. True, many are present here to-day who have been in the society for a comparatively short time. But the evolution of the society would be made impossible if we always had to begin at the beginning for those who enter newly; and on the other hand, to our great joy and satisfaction, large numbers of our oldest Anthroposophical friends have come here at this busy time when so many lecture-courses are to be given. Many Anthroposophists are gathered here who have witnessed nearly the whole period of Anthroposophical development and as time goes on opportunities must be created in the Anthroposophical Society for those in the earlier stages of membership to be properly introduced to all that must now be cultivated for the further course of the society's development.

I had to make these preliminary remarks, because what I shall say to-day will be given more in the form of a simple communication, and much of it may well appear exceedingly bold. It will however form the starting-point for what will follow in the succeeding lectures.

A human life after all only appears in its true nature when we consider how it passes through repeated lives on earth. Serious and responsible research in this domain is however by no means easy, for the results we gain do in a certain way contradict our habitual ideas on the subject.

At first sight, when considering the life of a man on earth with all the contents of his destiny, most people will be struck by those events of destiny which are connected with his outer profession or inner calling, with his social position and the like. As to the essential content of his earthly life, a human being will naturally appear to us in the light of these characteristics, nor need they by any means be superficial, for they may signify much for his inner life of soul. Nevertheless, to look into those depths in which repeated lives on earth are seen, it is necessary to look aside from many of these obvious and outer things that stamp themselves upon the destiny of a human being in his earthly life.

In effect, we must not imagine that the outer or inner calling of a man has a very great significance for his karma that passes through repeated lives on earth. True, even if we take

26

a comparatively external and typical calling, that of a civil servant for example, we can conceive how much it is connected, even outwardly, with his destiny. Nevertheless, for the deepest relationships of karma or destiny those things that we can describe in a man as proceeding from his external calling are sometimes of no significance at all. And so it is with inner callings too. How easily we are tempted, in the case of a musician, to think that at any rate in one former earthly life he was, if not a musician, an artist of some kind. But it is by no means always so. Nay, I must go farther—it is so only in the rarest cases. For when we investigate these things in reality, we find that the continued thread of karma or destiny goes far deeper into the inner being of man and is little connected with his outer profession or inner calling. It is far more concerned with the inner forces of soul and resistances of soul, with moral relationships which can, after all, reveal themselves in any and every calling whether it be an outer or an inner one.

For this very reason, the investigation of karma—of the thread of destiny—requires us to concentrate on circumstances in the life of a human being which may often appear outwardly trivial or of small importance. In this connection I must refer again and again to a fact that once occurred to me.

I had to investigate the karmic connections of a certain human being. He had many characteristics in this his present life. He had a certain task in life, he had indeed his profession. But to intuitive vision, from all that he did out of his profession, or that he did as a philanthropist and the like, no indication of his former earthly lives could be found. Not that these things were unconnected with his former lives on earth, but for spiritual vision they gave no clue. One could penetrate no farther when concentrating on these facts of his profession or of his philanthropic work. On the other hand, curiously enough, a quite unimportant peculiarity of his life gave a result. He frequently had to lecture. Every time before he began he quite habitually took out his pocket handkerchief and blew his nose! I often heard him lecture, and without exception whenever he began to speak (I do not mean when he began to speak in conversation, but whenever he had to speak continuously) he first took out his pocket-handkerchief and blew his nose. Now this gave a picture from which there radiated out the power to look into his former lives on earth.

I give this as a particularly grotesque example. It is not always so grotesque; but the point is, we must be able to enter into the whole human being if we wish to look in any valid way into his karma.

You see, from a deeper point of view, the special calling of a man is, after all, something that results from education and other circumstances. On the other hand, it is deeply connected with his inner spiritual configuration if every time before he begins to make a speech he simply cannot help taking out his pocket-handkerchief and blowing his nose! That is a thing far more intimately connected with the being of a man. Still, I admit, this is a radical and extreme example. It is not always quite like this. I wanted only to awaken in you the idea that for the investigation of karma, that which lies on the obvious surface of a man's life is as a rule of no use. We have to enter into certain intimate features of his life—I do not mean into things that one prys into unjustifiably—but into the finer qualities and characteristics that nevertheless appear quite openly.

Having said this by way of introduction, I will now relate a certain instance perfectly frankly and straightforwardly, and of course with all the reservations which are necessary in the case. I mean with the reservation that everyone is free to believe or disbelieve what I now say, though I must assure you that it is based on the deepest and most earnest spiritual-scientific research.

These things do not by any means come to one if one approaches them with the deliberate intention to investigate, like a modern scientist in his laboratory. In a certain way, researches on karma must themselves result from karma.

I had to mention this fact at the end of the new edition of my book *Theosophy*, for among the various strange requirements that have been made of me from time to time during my life, this too occurred not long ago.—It was suggested that I should submit myself to examination in some psychological laboratory, so that they might ascertain whether the things I have to say on spiritual science are well founded. It is of course just as absurd as if someone were to produce mathematical results and, instead of testing their accuracy, you were to challenge him to submit to an examination in a laboratory, to see whether or not he was a real mathematician. Absurdities of this kind go under the name of scholarship to-day and are taken seriously by learned people!

I said quite definitely at the close of the new edition of my *Theosophy* that experiments in this spirit can of course give no result. And I also mentioned that all the paths of approach which lead to the discovery of a certain occult result must themselves be prepared in a spiritual, in a supersensible way.

Now I once had occasion to meet an eminent doctor of our time, who was well known to me by reputation and especially by his literary career. I had a very high regard for him. You see, I am mentioning the karmic details which led to the investigation, the results of which I shall now describe. The investigation itself took a very long time and only reached its conclusion during the last few weeks. Only now has it reached a stage which enables me conscientiously to speak of it. I am mentioning all these details in order that you may see some at least of the inner connections, though of course not all of them.

Thus I made the acquaintance of this doctor, a man of our own day. When I met him I was in the company of another person whom I had known very well for a long time. This other person had always made, I will not say a deep, but a very thorough impression on me. He was exceedingly fond of the society of men who were interested in occultism in the widest possible range, though an occultism somewhat externally conceived. He was fond of relating the views of his many acquaintances on all kinds of occult matters, and especially on the occult connections of what the modern artist

29

should strive for, as a lyric and epic poet, or as a dramatist. Around this person there was what I might call a kind of moral, ethical aura. I am applying the word ' moral ' to all that is connected with the soul-qualities under the command of the will.

I was paying a visit to him, and in his company I found the other man first mentioned, whom I knew by reputation and respected very highly for his literary and medical career. Everything that took place during this visit made a deep impression on me and impelled me to receive the whole experience into the realm of spiritual research.

Then a very remarkable thing happened. By witnessing the two persons in the company of one another, and by the impression which my new acquaintance made on me—(I had known him for a long time as an eminent literary and medical man and had a great regard for him, but this was the first time that I saw him in the flesh)—by these impressions I gained certain perceptions. To begin with however, it enabled me, not to investigate in any way the connections in life and destiny of my new acquaintance. On the contrary, my seeing them together shed light as it were upon the other one, whom I had long known. And the result was this.—He had lived in ancient Egypt, not in his last, but in one of his former lives on earth. And (this is the peculiar thing) he had been mummified, embalmed as a mummy. Soon afterwards I discovered that the mummy was still in existence. Indeed a long time afterwards I saw the actual mummy. This, then, was the starting-point. But once the line of research had been kindled in connection with the person whom I had long known, it shed its light still farther, and eventually I was enabled to investigate the karmic connections of the other man, my new acquaintance, the doctor. And the following was the result.

As a general rule one is led from one earthly life of a human being to the preceding one. But in this case intuition led far back into ancient Egypt, to a kind of chieftain, and indeed to two personalities in ancient Egypt. It was a chieftain who in a certain sense, indeed in a very interesting way, possessed the ancient Egyptian Initiation, but had become somewhat decadent as an Initiate. In the further course of his life, he began to take his Initiation not very seriously, indeed he even treated it with a certain scorn. Now this man had a servant, who in his turn was extremely serious. This servant was of course not initiated; but both of them together were given the task of embalming mummies and procuring the substances for this purpose, which was no easy matter.

Now especially in the more ancient periods of Egypt, the process of embalming mummies was very complicated and demanded an intimate knowledge of the human being, of the human body. Nay more, of those who had to do the embalming—if they did it legitimately—deep knowledge of the human soul was required. The chieftain of whom I spoke had been initiated for this very work, but he gradually became, in a manner of speaking, frivolous in relation to this, his proper calling. So it came about that in the course of time he betrayed (so they would have put it in the language of the Mysteries) the knowledge he had received through his Initiation to his servant, and the latter gradually proved to be a man who understood the content of Initiation better than the Initiate himself. Thus the servant became the embalmer of mummies, and at length his master did not even trouble to supervise the work, though of course he still took advantage of the social position, etc., which this honourable task involved. But at length his character became such that he no longer enjoyed great respect, and he thus came into various conflicts of life. The servant, on the other hand, worked his way up by degrees to a very, very earnest conception of life, and was thus taken hold of, in a remarkably congenial way, by a kind of Initiation. It was no *real* Initiation, but it lived within him instinctively. Thus a large number of mummies were mummified under the supervision and co-operation of these two people.

Time went on. The two men passed through the gate of death and underwent the experiences of which I shall speak next time—the experiences in the supersensible which are connected with the development of karma or destiny. And in the Roman epoch they both of them came back to earthly life. They came back at the very time when the dominion of the Roman Emperors was founded, in the time of Augustus —not exactly, but approximately, in the time of Augustus himself.

I said above that this is a matter of conscientious research, no less exact in its methods than any researches of physics or chemistry, and I should not speak of these things unless for some weeks past it had become possible for me to speak of them so definitely.

The chieftain, who had gradually become a really frivolous Initiate, and who, when he had passed through the gate of death, had felt this as an extraordinarily bitter trial of earthly life, experiencing it in all the bitterness of its effects—we find him again as Julia, the daughter of Augustus. She married Tiberius, the step-son of Augustus, and led a life which to herself seemed justified but was considered, in the Roman society of that time, so immoral that at length both she and Tiberius were banished.

The other man—the servant who had worked his way from the bottom upwards nearly to the grade of an Initiate—was born again at the same time, as the Roman historian, *Titus Livius*, or Livy.

It is most interesting how Livy came to be an historian. In the ancient Egyptian times he had embalmed a large number of mummies. The souls who had lived in the bodies of these mummies—very many of them—were reincarnated as Romans. And certain ones among them were actually reincarnated as the seven Kings of Rome. For the Seven Kings were no mere legendary figures. Going back into the time when the chieftain and his servant had lived in Egypt, we come into a very old Egyptian epoch. Now through a certain law which applies especially to the reincarnation of souls whose bodies have been mummified, these souls were called back again to earth comparatively soon. And the karmic connection of the servant of the chieftain with the souls whose bodies he had embalmed was so intimate, that

32

he had to write the history of the very same human beings who in a previous life he had embalmed, though naturally, he also included the history of many others whom he had not embalmed. Thus Titus Livius became an historian. Now I would like some, indeed as many of you as possible, to take Livy's Roman History, and, with the knowledge that results from these karmic connections, to receive a real impression of his style. You will see that his peculiar penetration into the human being and his tendency at the same time towards the style of the myth, is akin to that intimate knowledge of man which an embalmer could attain.

We do not perceive such connections until the corresponding researches have been made. But once this has been done, a great light is shed on many things. It is difficult to understand the origin of the peculiar style of Titus Livius, who as it were embalms the human beings whom he describes. For such is his style. Real light is thrown upon it when we point to these connections.

Thus we have the same two people again as Julia and Titus Livius. Then Julia and Livy passed once more through the gate of death. The one soul had had the experience of being an Initiate to a considerable degree, and having then distorted his Initiation by frivolous conduct. He had discovered all the bitterness of the after-effects of this in the life between death and a new birth. He had then undergone a peculiar destiny in his new life on earth as Julia, of which life you may read in history. The result was, that in his next life between death and a new birth (following on the life as Julia) he conceived a strong antipathy to this his incarnation as Julia. And in a curious way this antipathy of his was universalised. For spiritual intuition shows this individuality in his life between death and a new birth as though perpetually crying out: " Would that I had never become a woman! It was the evil that I did in yonder life in ancient Egypt which led me thus to become a woman."

We can now trace the life of these two individualities still farther. We come into the Middle Ages. We find Livy again as the glad poet and minstrel in the very centre of the Middle

33

Ages. We are astonished to find him thus, for there is no connection between the external callings. But the greatest possible surprises that a human being can possibly have are those that result from a real study of successive lives on earth. The Roman historian, with his style that proceeded from a knowledge of man acquired in embalming mummies, with his style so wonderfully light—we find him again as the poet *Walther von der Vogelweide*. His style is carried upwards, as it were, upon the wings of lyric poetry.

Walther von der Vogelweide lived in the Tyrol. He had many patrons; and among his many patrons there was one very peculiar man, who was on familiar terms with alchemists of every kind, for there were scores of alchemists at that time, in the Tyrol. This man was himself the owner of a castle, but he frequented all manner of alchemists' dens and hovels. In so doing he learned extraordinarily much, and (as happened in the case of Paracelsus too) by spending his time in the dens of alchemists he was impelled to study all occult matters very intensely, and gained an unusually intense feeling for occult things. He thus came into the position of rediscovering in the Tyrol what was then only known as a legend, namely, the Castle in the Mountain—the Castle in the Rocks—(which indeed no one would have recognised as such, for it consisted of rocks, it was hollowed out of the rocks)—I mean, the Castle of the Dwarf King Laurin. The daemonic nature in the district of the Castle of the Dwarf King Laurin made a profound impression on him. Thus there was a remarkable combination in this soul—Initiation which he had carried into frivolity, annoyance at having been a woman and having thus been drawn into the sphere of Roman immorality and, at the same time, Roman cant and hypocrisy about morals; and lastly, an intimate knowledge, though still only external, of all manner of alchemical matters, which knowledge he had extended to a clear feeling of the nature-daemons and of other spiritual agencies in nature.

These two men—though it is not recorded in the biography of Walther, nevertheless it is the case—Walther von der

34

Vogelweide and this other man often came together, and Walther received many an influence and impulse from him.

Here we have an instance of what is really a kind of karmic law. We see the same people drawn together again and again, called to the earth again and again simultaneously, complementing one another, living in a kind of mutual contrast. It is interesting once more, to enter into the peculiar lyrical style of Walther. It is as though at last he had grown thoroughly sick of embalming dead mummies and had turned to an entirely different aspect of life. He will no longer have anything to do with dead things, but only with the fullness and joy of life. And yet again, there is a certain undercurrent of pessimism in his work. Feel the style of Walther von der Vogelweide, feel in his style the two preceding earthly lives: feel too, his restless life. It is extraordinarily reminiscent of that life which dawns upon one who spends much of his time with the dead, when many destinies are unburdened in the soul. For such indeed was the case with an embalmer of mummies.

Now we go on.—My further researches into this karmic chain led me at length into the same room where I had visited my old acquaintance, whom I had recognised as an Egyptian mummy. And now I perceived that this very mummy had been embalmed by the other man whom I now met in his room. The whole line of research led me back to this same room. In effect, I found the soul who had passed through the servant of the old Egyptian embalmer, through Titus Livius, through Walther von der Vogelweide—I found him again in the doctor of our time, in *Ludwig Schleich*.

Thus astonishingly do the connections in life appear. Who, with the ordinary consciousness alone, can understand an earthly life? It *can* only be understood when we know what is there in the foundations of a soul. Theoretically, many people know that deep in the foundations of the soul there are the layers of successive earthly lives. But it becomes real and concrete only when we behold it in a specific instance.

Then inner vision was directed out of this room once more. (For in the case of the other man, who had been mummified

35

by this one, I was led to no more clues—at any rate to no important ones.) On the other hand I now perceived the further soul-pilgrimage of the old chieftain, of Julia, of the discoverer of Laurin's Castle. For he came back to earth as *August Strindberg*.

Now I would like you to take the whole life and literary work of August Strindberg and set it against the background which I have just described. See the peculiar misogyny of Strindberg, which is no true misogyny, but proceeds from quite different foundations. Look, too, at all the strange daemonic elements that occur in his works. See his peculiar attraction to all manner of alchemistic and occult arts and artifices. And at length, look at the adventurous life of August Strindberg. You will find how well it stands out against the background which I have described.

Then read the Memoirs of Ludwig Schleich, his relations to August Strindberg, and you will see how all this arises once more against the background of their former earthly lives. Indeed, from the Memoirs of Ludwig Schleich a very remarkable light may suddenly arise, a light truly astonishing. For the man in whose company I first met Ludwig Schleich—the man of whom I said that in his ancient Egyptian life he was mummified by Schleich—it is he of whom Schleich himself tells in his Memoirs that he led him to Strindberg. In a past life, Strindberg and Schleich had worked together upon the corpse. And the soul who dwelt in that body, led them together again.

Thus, all that we have to explain to begin with about re-peated earthly lives and the karmic connections in general, becomes real and concrete. Only then do the facts that appear in earthly life become transparent. A single human life on earth is an entire mystery. What else can it be, until seen against the background of the former lives on earth?

My dear friends, when I explain such things as these I always have an accompanying feeling. If these things which it has become possible to set forth since the Christmas Foundation Meeting are to be regarded in a true sense they demand real earnestness in the listener. They demand an earnest spirit. They require us to stand with real earnestness in the Anthroposophical Movement. For they might easily lead to all manner of frivolities. But they are brought forward here because it is necessary for the Anthroposophical Society to-day to take its stand on a basis of real earnestness and to become conscious of its tasks in modern civilisation.

Having thus laid the foundation, I wish to speak in the next lecture about the karma of the Anthroposophical Society. And in the following lecture which I shall then announce, I shall pass on to describe what these studies of karma may become for the human being who wishes to understand his own life in its deeper meaning.

Lecture 3

We understand only the very smallest part of human history and of our own life if we consider it in its external aspect, I mean in that aspect which we see from the limited view-point of our earthly life between birth and death. It is impossible to comprehend the inner motives of history and life unless we turn our gaze to that spiritual background which underlies the outer, physical happenings. Men do indeed describe as history the events that take place in the physical world, and they often say that this world-history represents causes and effects. Thus they will approach the events of the second decade of the 20th century, describing them as the effects of events in the first decade and so forth. Yet how is so great an illusion possible ? It is as though we saw a running stream of water throwing waves up on to the surface and tried to explain each successive wave as the result of the preceding one, whereas the forces bringing forth the waves are really penetrating upwards from below. So it is indeed. That which takes place at any point of historic evolution or of human life in general is moulded out of the spiritual world, and as to these events we can speak of causes and effects only to a very slight extent.

I will show you by a whole series of examples how we must include the spiritual events along with the external happenings in order to gain a true picture of what underlies the latter.

Our present age in its spiritual aspects is connected, as you know, with what is called in spiritual life, the dominion of Michael, and this dominion of Michael is connected in turn with what the Anthroposophical Movement in the deepest sense intends, with what this movement ought to be and do. Thus the events of which I shall speak are not unconnected, as we shall see next time, with the destiny, the karma of the Anthroposophical Society, and hence too with the karma of the great majority of the individual human beings who find themselves within this society.*

Some of the things on which I shall touch this evening are already known to you from earlier lectures. But to-day I wish to consider from a certain point of view the known and the, as yet, unknown together. Since the Mystery of Golgotha we see a continuous stream of Christian evolution passing through the civilised world. I have often described the directions taken by this Christian evolution in the successive centuries. But it is also not be denied that many other influences entered into this stream of Christian evolution. For had this not been so, the civilisation of our present time could not be permeated by that intense materialism by which it is in fact permeated.

True, it cannot be denied that the Christian creeds and confessions themselves have contributed not a little to this materialism. Yet they have done so not out of truly Christian impulses but out of other impulses which entered the stream of Christian evolution from altogether different quarters.

Let us take a certain period—the 8th and the beginning of the 9th century A.D. We see the personality of Charlemagne, for instance, carrying Christianity in all directions among the non-Christian peoples who were still living in Europe at that time, though he does so by methods of which we with our present humanitarian ideas cannot always approve.

Now among the non-Christian people of that time those especially are interesting who were influenced by the streams that came over from Asia through northern Africa to Europe, proceeding from Arabism and Mohammedanism. In this connection we must understand Mohammedanism in the wider sense of the term.

Something over 500 years after the Mystery of Golgotha we see the rise of all the old elements of Arabian world-conception in Arabism, Mohammedanism and much that was connected with these. We see above all a rich and varied scholarship, but a scholarship that was given an unchristian

* See Rudolf Steiner, *The Karmic Relationships of the Anthroposophical Movement*. Vol. III in this series.

shape. We see all this spread out of Asia by powerful and warlike campaigns through northern Africa to the west and south of Europe. Then gradually this stream dies away and is lost so far as the more outer world is concerned. But it by no means dies away in the inward development of the spiritual life. When the more external spread of Arabism into Europe is already dying out, we see this same Arabism continuing to spread in a more inward way. This is one of the places where we have to look from external history towards the spiritual background. You will remember what I said in our last lecture on karma, that in considering the successive earthly lives of individual human beings, we cannot draw conclusions from the external attitude and features of a man as to the nature of his former life on earth. It is the more deeply inward impulses that matter. Thus it is with the important person-alities of history—it is the more inward impulses that matter.

We see the results of former civilisation-epochs carried into later ones by the personalities of history, i.e., by the human beings themselves, but we also see them changing in the process. And by studying the external aspect we may not immediately recognise these impulses in the new form in which a human being carries and expresses them in a new incarnation. Let us now consider a deeply inward stream of this kind.

When Charlemagne was spreading Christianity—if we may say so, in a somewhat primitive manner—in the then primi-tive civilisation of Europe, there lived in the East a per-sonality who stood really on a far greater height of culture, I mean *Haroun al Raschid.*

At his court in Asia Minor, Haroun al Raschid gathered the most eminent spiritual and intellectual figures of his time. Illustrious was the court of Haroun al Raschid, and held in high esteem even by Charlemagne himself. Architec-ture, poetry, astrology, geography, history, anthropology—all of these were brilliantly represented by the most illustrious of men. Some of these men still carried in them much of the knowledge of ancient Initiation-Science.

Haroun al Raschid himself was an organiser in the grandest

style. He was able to make a kind of universal academy of his court where the several departments of what the East at that time possessed in art and science were joined into a great organic whole. And side by side with him there stood above all one other personality, who truly bore within him the elements of ancient Initiation.

It is indeed not the case that an Initiate of a former incarnation must necessarily appear as an Initiate in a later. You may indeed raise the question, my dear friends, for it is suggested by many things that have been stated in these lectures: Were there not Initiates in ancient time? Where then have they gone? Have they not been reincarnated? Where are they to-day? Where were they in recent centuries? They were here indeed but we must bear in mind that one who was an Initiate in a former incarnation must above all make use in a later incarnation of that external bodily nature which the new age can provide. And the recent evolution of mankind provides no bodies so plastic, so soft and mobile that that which lived in such an individuality in a former incarnation can come to light in them directly. Thus the Initiates receive quite different tasks in which what they had in their former Initiation does indeed work unconsciously, in the power of the impulses they give, but does not appear in the outer form of the working of an Initiate.

Thus at the Court of Haroun al Raschid there lived a certain counsellor, a second organiser by his side, who possessed an extraordinarily deep insight, though it was not in that incarnation the direct insight of an Initiate. He rendered the very greatest service to Haroun al Raschid.

These two men, Haroun al Raschid and his counsellor, went through the gate of death, and having arrived yonder in the spiritual realm, they still witnessed as it were the final phases of the spread of Arabism, on the one hand through Africa to Spain and thence far into Europe, and on the other hand into Central Europe. They were great powers, these two individualities, and Haroun al Raschid did many things during that life contributing to the spread of Arabism here in the physical world.

Indeed Arabism had taken on a peculiar form at the court of Haroun al Raschid. It was a form proceeding in its turn from many and varied formations which art and science had received for a long time past in Asia. The last great wave of evolution towards Asia had gone forth from the preceding age of Michael. It was the Grecian spiritual life, the Grecian spirituality and artistic sense, synthesised in the community of Alexander the Great and Aristotle. The flower of the Grecian spiritual life had been carried across to Asia and Africa by Alexander the Great with extraordinary impetus and energy, yet at the same time in a way that was exemplary for the spreading of a spiritual impulse. All this was permeated with the spirit which found its scientific expression in Aristotelianism in Asia Minor and Africa. Thus we may say in general that the mind of Arabism and Orientalism was shaped and permeated by those impulses which ancient Greece brought forth in Aristotle and which were spread into the world so brilliantly by Alexander. We look back even several centuries before the Mystery of Golgotha. We look back to the campaigns of Alexander the Great where the treasures of wisdom to which I just referred were spread far and wide. And from that time throughout the centuries down to Haroun al Raschid who lived in the 8th century A.D., we find in Asia a mind and a receptiveness for Grecian spiritual life in its Aristotelian form. Nevertheless this spiritual life had taken on a peculiar shape there. Powerful as it was, magnificent and penetrating, deeply united with Arabism and permeating it, this Aristotelianism, this Alexandrianism that flourished at the court of Haroun al Raschid and was cultivated by him and his counsellor and those around them, nay more, that was even permeated there by ancient oriental wisdom of Initiation, it was not that genuine spiritual life which had been cultivated as between Aristotle and Alexander themselves, for example. It had taken on forms which were little inclined to enter into Christianity. Thus yonder in Asia we see a certain Aristotelianism and Alexandrianism, brilliantly cultivated under the aegis of Haroun al Raschid and his counsellor. It represented one pole of Aristotle, that pole which is averse to Christianity, which took on a spiritual form (above all a kind of Pantheism), but which by its very essence never would nor could unite with Christianity.

With this tendency of an ancient spiritual life that would not enter into Christianity, Haroun al Raschid and his counsellor went through the gate of death. And having gone through the gate of death, all their effort, all their longing, all their power was directed from the spiritual world to continue as it were to play a part in historic evolution in the spreading of the spiritual life of Arabism from Asia into Europe, thus continuing what had formerly been achieved by warlike and other methods. From the spiritual world after their death they sent down spiritual rays, as it were, intended to penetrate Europe in its spiritual life with Arabism.

Thus we see Haroun al Raschid taking the following spiritual line of development after his death, watching with interest all that took place for the spread of Arabism from Asia Minor through the South of Europe and through Spain—watching it and continuing it further. And correspondingly (for the human being living in the spiritual world partakes in a sense in what is here below in the physical)—the other man took a different path in the spiritual world which in its projection would appear as a more northerly line, from the Black Sea towards Middle Europe. Thus, we may turn and look upward to these two individualities, following them as it were in their spirit-wanderings which may indeed be thus projected down on to the physical plane.

Now you know how Aristotelianism, Alexandrianism, had spread and entered even historically into Christianity. In the 9th, 10th, 11th, 12th and even into the 13th century, one of the most popular subjects of narrative everywhere in Europe was that connected with Alexander the Great. Thus we have the wonderful poem, the " Song of Alexander " by the priest Lamprecht, extolling the works of Alexander but connecting them everywhere with the spiritual world. He describes the education of Alexander, his life, his campaigns into Asia, and everywhere he brings out what was living spiritually in this

44

earthly life of Alexander. For as we know, all earthly life is connected with spiritual things, only the ordinary consciousness does not see it. All these spiritual elements were contained in the medieval treatment of the subject. So too, Aristotelianism spread in Christian Europe even into scholasticism. We find Aristotelian concepts everywhere, only it is the other pole of Aristotelianism. Yonder in Asia it was in an Arabist form; here in Europe, in a Christian. The "Song of Alexander" is permeated through and through by a Christian spirit, and Aristotelianism too was cultivated in Europe in an essentially Christian form.

Nay more, we find this extraordinary process: the Christian doctors of the Church, their souls equipped with Aristotle, battling against those who had carried the other Aristotle across from Asia into Spain, spreading an unchristian doctrine. On all hands we see the conflict of Aristotelianism in the Christian fathers of the Church, we see it in the pictures that were painted in a later time, the Church fathers holding in their hand what they had gained from Aristotle, and treading under foot Averröes and the others who stood for their kind of Aristotelianism that had come through Alexandrianism into Europe. This was taking place externally. But at the same time, if we may describe it out of spiritual research, Haroun al Raschid and his counsellor lived on, having passed through the gate of death as I just indicated, and needless to say, Alexander and Aristotle themselves lived on. Once only they paid as it were a fleeting visit to the earth in the first Christian centuries in a district not without interest for the Anthroposophical Movement. Then they returned again into the spiritual world and they were together in the spiritual world at a certain time after Haroun al Raschid and his counsellor had left the physical plane once more. They themselves, the real individualities of Aristotle and Alexander, took different paths from Haroun al Raschid and his counsellor. For they went forward with the Christian evolution. They went westward with the evolution of Christianity.

And now the most important and essential events took place in the 9th century. And this is the extraordinary thing.

45

The event which from the spiritual world was of the greatest importance for the spiritual development in Europe, coincided in the supersensible worlds with an external event in which it is by no means easy to recognise it. Nevertheless it coincided. In the very year A.D. 869 something of immense significance took place in the spiritual worlds, while down below the 8th Oecumenical Council was taking place in Constantinople where it was declared dogmatically that one must not say, if one would be a true Christian, that man consists of body, soul and spirit. Trichotomy, as it was called, was declared heretical. I have often referred to this fact before and expressed it in these words, that in the Council of A.D. 869 the spirit was abolished. Thenceforth one was bound to say: man consists of body and soul, and the soul has certain spiritual qualities. Now what took place in this way down below in Constantinople was the earthly projection of a spiritual event—an event which men do not recognise but which was of immense significance for European spiritual history, an event extending over many years, which can, however, be dated to this very year.

In the 9th century the time had already come when European humanity, even in its spiritual life, had altogether forgotten what had been quite familiar to the true Christians in the first Christian centuries, I mean that Christ was a Being who had formerly been in the Sun, whose life had been connected with the Sun, and who had then incarnated in the body of Jesus of Nazareth, as we have often described at this place. This knowledge was familiar to the earliest Christians, the knowledge of Christ as the Sun Being, as a Being connected with the cosmic world through His dwelling in the Sun before the Mystery of Golgotha: the Christ not only as the Sun Being but as the Being united with all the planetary existence that is connected with the Sun.

But this cosmic origin of the Christ Impulse was no longer known in the 9th century. The full greatness of the Christ Impulse had as it were been put aside. Nearer and nearer men approached what was called the purely human, that is to say, what takes place on the physical plane alone. They

46

no longer explained in the Gospels that which points out into the Cosmos, but they took the content of the Gospels and told it like an earthly epic narrative. Really to understand what this change signified we must bear in mind that in the true evolution of mankind there was indeed a Christianity before Christ, before the Mystery of Golgotha. We must take in real earnestness such words as those of St. Augustine who declared: Christianity was always there, only those who were Christians before the Mystery of Golgotha were called by other names.

This saying is indeed only the outer expression of something of immense and deep significance. Everywhere in the true Mysteries, nay even in those places which though not in themselves the Mysteries, were permeated by knowledge and impulses from the Mysteries, there was indeed a Christianity before the Mystery of Golgotha. Only they spoke of the Christ Being as of a Being who is in the Sun, and whom one can behold and with whom one can work when through the wisdom of Initiation one has reached the point at which the real Sun life in its spiritual content is actually present to one.

Thus in the ancient Mysteries they spoke of the Christ who was to come. They spoke not of an earthly Christ who had lived or who was present on the earth, but they spoke of the Coming Christ who would be here in the future and whom they still sought for in the Sun.

Now even in later times such knowledge and tradition continued and entered into certain places which Christianity had not yet reached even in the centuries after the life of Christ.

During our recent stay in England during the Summer Course* at Torquay in the West of England, not far from the place† where Arthur was with his followers once upon a time (we were able to visit this actual place), a result of spiritual research was given to me, pointing to a belated working of

* See *True and False Paths in Spiritual Investigation*, 2nd Edition 1969, Rudolf Steiner Press, London.
† Tintagel, North Cornwall.

this kind in a pre-Christian Christianity. For at this place it had indeed been preserved into a far later time. The content of the King Arthur Legend referred to later times by a scholarship which is not at all scholarly in respect of the real facts, reaches back in reality into a very early epoch, and it is indeed a deep impression which one may receive when one stands at that place, looking down into the sea, even as once upon a time the Knights of the Round Table looked out upon the sea from there. Even to-day, if one is receptive to these things, one receives a very real impression which tells one what it was that the Knights of the Round Table of King Arthur did in their gigantic castle. The last relics of the castle, the crumbling stones, the latest witnesses to its existence, stand there to this day. Gigantic is the impression of this place of ruins, entirely broken down as it is, and from there one looks out into the ocean. It is a mountainous promontory with the sea on either side. The weather changes almost hour by hour. We look out into the sea and watch the glittering sunshine reflected in the water. Then the next moment there is wind and tempest. Looking with occult vision at what takes place there to this day, we receive a magnificent impression. There live and weave the elemental spirits evolving out of the activities of the light and air, and of the foaming waves of the sea that turn and beat upon the shore. The life and movement and interplay of these elemental spirits gives even to-day a vivid and direct impression of how the sun works in its own nature in the earth, and meets with that which grows forth from the earth below by way of powers and spirits of the Elements. There we receive even to-day the impression: such was the immediate original source of inspiration of the twelve who belonged to King Arthur. We see them standing there, these Knights of the Round Table, watching the play of the powers of light and air, water and earth, the elemental spirits. We see too how these elemental spirits were messengers to them, bringing to them the messages from sun and moon and stars which entered into the impulses of their work, especially in the more ancient time. And much of this was preserved through the centuries of the post-Christian time, even into the 9th century of which I was just speaking.

It was the task of the Order of King Arthur, founded in that region by the instructions of Merlin, to cultivate and civilise Europe at a time when all Europe in its spiritual life stood under the influence of the strangest elemental beings. More than will be believed to-day, the ancient life of Europe needs to be comprehended in this sense. We must see in it on all hands the working of elementary spiritual beings, right into the life of man.

The Arthurian life, as I said, goes back into pre-Christian times, and before the Gospel came there, even in its oldest forms, there lived in it the knowledge, at any rate the practical instinctive knowledge of Christ as the Sun Spirit, before the Mystery of Golgotha. And in all that the Knights of the Round Table of King Arthur did, this same *Cosmic Christ* was living, the Christ who though not under the name of Christ, was also living in the impetus with which Alexander the Great had carried the Grecian culture and spiritual life into Asia. There were, so to speak, later ' campaigns of Alexander ' undertaken by the Knights of the Round Table of King Arthur into Europe, even as the real campaigns of Alexander had gone from Macedonia to Asia.

I mention this as an example, which could be investigated in the most recent times, to show how the worship of the sun, that is to say, the ancient worship of the Christ, was cultivated in such a place, though needless to say it was the Christ as He was for men before the Mystery of Golgotha. There all things were cosmic, even to the transition of the cosmos into the earthly Elements, the elemental spirits who lived in light and air and water and in the earth, for even in these there lived the cosmic forces. It was not possible at that time in the knowledge of these Elements to deny the cosmic principle that they contained. Thus even in the 9th century, in the paganism of Europe, there still lived much of the pre-Christian Christianity. That is the remarkable fact. More-over even in that time the belated followers of European paganism understood the Cosmic Christ far more worthily and truly than those who received the Christ in the Christianity that was spread officially under that name. Strangely we can see the life around King Arthur radiate into the present time, continued even into our time, placed into the immediate present by the sudden power of destiny. Thus I beheld in seership a member of the Round Table of King Arthur, who lived the life of the Round Table in a very deep and intense way, though he stood a little aside from the others who were given more to the adventures of their knighthood. This was a knight who lived a rather contemplative life, though it was not like the Knighthood of the Grail, for this did not exist in Arthur's circle. What the knights did in the fulfilment of their tasks, which in accordance with that age were for the most part warlike campaigns, was called by the name ' Adventure ' (Aventure). But there was one who stood out from among the others as I saw him, revealing a life truly wonderful in its inspiration. For we must imagine the knights going out on to the spur of land, seeing the wonderful play of clouds above, the waves beneath, the surging interplay of the one and the other, which gives a mighty and majestic impression to this very day. In all this they saw the Spiritual and were inspired with it, and this gave them their strength. But there was one among them who penetrated most deeply into this surging and foaming of the waves, with the spiritual beings wildly rising in the foam with their figures grotesque to earthly sight. He had a wonderful perception of the way in which the marvellously pure sun-influence played into the rest of nature, living and weaving in the spiritual life and movement of the surface of the ocean. He saw what lived in the light nature of the sun, borne up as it were by the watery atmosphere as we can see to this day, the sunlight approaching the trees and the spaces between the trees quite differently than in other regions, glittering back from between the trees, and playing often as in rainbow colours. Such a knight there was among them, one who had a peculiarly penetrating vision of these things. I was much concerned to follow his life into later time to see the individuality again. For just in this case something would needs enter into a later

50

incarnation of a Christian life that was almost primitive and pagan, that was Christian only to the extent that I have just described. And this in fact was what appeared, for that Knight of the Round Table of King Arthur was born again as Arnold Böcklin. This riddle which had followed me for an immensely long time, can only be solved in connection with the Round Table of King Arthur.

Thus you see that we have a Christianity tangible with spiritual touch to this very day, a Christianity before the Mystery of Golgotha which shed its light even into the time that I have just outlined.

Now while the 8th Oecumenical Council was being held in Constantinople, the human beings who had gone through the gate of death, and who knew well what had been the Christianity before the Mystery of Golgotha, met together, if I may put it so, in a simultaneous heavenly council in which Aristotle, Alexander, Haroun al Raschid and his counsellor, and many of the circle of the Round Table of King Arthur, were foregathered.

There they were at pains to overcome the Arabism living in the individualities of Haroun al Raschid and the other— to overcome it by the Christian impulses that lived in the will of Alexander and Aristotle. But this did not succeed. The individualities were ill-adapted to it.

There was, however, another result of that heavenly council. Thenceforth the ancient Cosmic Christianity lived still more deeply in the human beings who came from the Round Table of King Arthur than in their former, more rough-and-ready attitudes as Knights of King Arthur. And in that council that was held above the earth, face to face with what was likely then to happen in the future, which they could foresee through the Michael power that was working with them, Alexander and Aristotle made their resolutions so to speak, resolving how the spiritual life in Europe was to receive the new impulses of a Christianised Alexandrianism and Aristotelianism. But Haroun al Raschid and his counsellor adhered to their old ways. Now it is of the greatest significance to trace the further development in

European spiritual history of what had taken place in that heavenly council, if I may call it so. For looking at their further wanderings in the spiritual life, we find that the great organiser Haroun al Raschid who had lived so mightily on earth in the time of Charlemagne, returns again. He appears at a later time in the very midst of Christendom, but he has taken his Arabism with him through the life between death and a new birth. Nor need it be outwardly similar to the Arabic element in its outward configuration as it appears again in the physical world. It clothes itself in the new forms, the while in these new forms it still remains in essence the old, the Mohammedanism and Arabism. It appears again, active and effective in the European spiritual life, inasmuch as Haroun al Raschid is reincarnated in *Francis Bacon of Verulam*.

And it appears once more in a different way, even very strangely permeated with Christianity, inasmuch as Haroun al Raschid's counsellor is born again in Central Europe, and carries his influence far and wide in Europe as *Amos Comenius*. Much in the spiritual life of Europe took place in connection with what the resurrected spirits of the Court of Haroun al Raschid in these two human figures founded in Europe.

All this had first been prepared before it took place in actuality; for that which afterwards came forth in Francis Bacon and Comenius had been working spiritually from the spiritual world for a long time, and it had taken on the most intense forms as a result of the heavenly council of 869. And against it there now worked the other pole, the pole which had accepted Alexandrianism and Aristotelianism for the stream of Christianity. It was expressed in the most manifold influences which worked themselves out in lonely centres of cultivation of Christian spiritual life.

We recognise one such centre especially in the School of Chartres* to which I have now often referred in the hearing of some though not of all who are present to-day. The School of Chartres which flourished especially in the 12th century,

* See *The Karmic Relationships of the Anthroposophical Movement*.

contained a mighty spiritual impulse. Sylvester of Chartres, Alanus ab Insulis and other spirits who taught like these two, or who were otherwise connected with the school, had very much in them of the ancient wisdom of Initiation. And though they themselves could not be called Initiates in the full and true sense of the word, nevertheless there was much within them of the old wisdom of Initiation. The books which they produced look like long catalogues of words, but at that time it was not possible to express in any other way what one wished to give in fullness of life in bocks. It had to be in the fullness of rhetoric as a kind of catalogue of words. He however who knows how to read will perceive very much in these books of what was taught in a most wonderful way to many pupils spiritually permeated by the great teachers of Chartres.

Truly a wonderful spiritual star shone over the spiritual life of Europe in that School of Chartres, where to this day there stand the wonderful architectural forms of the Cathedral, revealing most beautifully the work of many centuries. In other places too, this spiritual life was living. It was a spiritual life working in spiritual ways and giving an altogether different and more spiritual insight into nature than that which afterwards came to take its place. It is interesting to see the manifold ways in which that spiritual life rayed out. In France, in one place after another we can see how even in the teaching that was given, the spirit of Chartres lived on in the High Schools carried over into Southern France, and even into Italy. But it lived not only in the teachings, it lived on in an immediately spiritual way. Interesting it is how Brunetto Latini, having been an Ambassador in Spain during a certain time, returned to Florence, the city of his fathers, heard of its misfortune even from a distance, and thus suffered a powerful convulsion of his soul, to which was added a slight attack of sunstroke. In this bodily condition the human being is easily accessible to spiritual influences that work in a spiritual way. It is indeed well known how Brunetto Latini on his way to Florence experienced what was actually a kind of elementary initiation. Brunetto Latini became Dante's teacher, and the spirituality of the *Commedia* proceeds from the teachings which Brunetto Latini gave to his pupil Dante.

In all this there lives what was agreed supersensibly, if I may put it so, in the spiritual Council of 869. For the inspiration of the teachings of Chartres, the inspiration of Brunetto Latini, and even the inspiration of Dante, enabling cosmic things to live in Dante's poem—all these things are connected with the impulse that proceeded from that supersensible Congress in the 9th century A.D.

We must see all these things together, the spiritual life of Europe from the old time of Alexander, in the time of the Mystery of Golgotha, in the time of the School of Chartres; and we shall see how we can trace it still farther into the later time. We must see in their mutual interplay that which takes place in the supersensible and its shadowed image down here in the physical world. Then only do we really begin to understand what must be called the stream of Michael to-day, and what this stream of Michael to-day intends.

Then we can penetrate and see what is the will of the Anthroposophical Movement according to the stream of Michael. We shall say more of this in the next lectures.

Lecture 4

If we wish our human thought and action to be permeated once more by spiritual life, it will be necessary to receive again in full earnestness such conceptions of the spiritual world as have passed through our souls in these last lectures. For many centuries these conceptions have in reality been lacking to mankind and notably to civilised mankind.

Looking back into various epochs of human history we shall find how in earlier ages human action upon earth was everywhere connected with what was taking place in the supersensible. It is not that a consciousness of the super-sensible—a certain abstract consciousness of it—has been lacking to the greater part of mankind in recent times. No—but the courage has been lacking to attach the concrete deeds and happenings in the earthly sphere to the equally real forms of life and movement in spiritual worlds.

With our recent studies we are coming to do this once more. And we do so especially when we bring the earthly life of men, as we have been doing here, into connection with the life between death and a new birth, when we connect what is taking place in one earthly life with that which is accomplished in the successive lives of man.

We have begun to consider that spiritual, supersensible stream of which I was allowed to say that it is connected with our present stream of Michael in the service of which Anthroposophy has placed itself. We have thus entered upon the path which in a certain sense is to approach the karma of the Anthroposophical Movement itself, and at the same time, the karma of the individuals who unite the life of their soul and spirit sincerely, out of a straightforward inner impulse, with the Anthroposophical Movement.

I told you of a supersensible event which took place under the aegis as it were of the Michael Power at the very time when the Council of 869 was taking place on earth. We know how deeply the whole life and civilisation of the Middle Ages was influenced by that Council. We need only watch the deep reserve with which enlightened spirits in the Middle Ages avoid speaking of the threefold human being, of body, soul and spirit. For the 8th Oecumenical Council at Constantinople had declared the doctrine of the threefold man heretical. Considering the power of such edicts in the Middle Ages it is quite clear that the whole of the spiritual life here on earth then had to take its course as it were under the shadow of this declaration which condemned Trichotomy as heretical.

But all the more intense was that spiritual life which has been working for a long time preparing the Michael stream for the 20th century, the Michael stream in which we stand since the last third of the 19th century and in which mankind will be for three or four centuries to come.

To-day we will speak of the course of this stream of Michael to which we have already begun to turn attention. Then, next Sunday, we shall approach more nearly matters connected on the one hand with the karma of the Anthroposophical Movement, and on the other hand karmically with the spiritual and intellectual life of the present time.

I told you of a kind of supersensible Council which took place in spiritual regions over the earth at the same time as the 8th Oecumenical Council in Constantinople. In that spiritual council there met together the individualities of Haroun al Raschid and of his wise counsellor, and also the individualities of Alexander and Aristotle. Moreover there were also gathered there the individualities from the time of the spiritual service of King Arthur; and as I explained, all this took place under the aegis of Michael.

Then I told you how Haroun al Raschid appeared again, bringing with him into Europe an oriental spiritual life with an Aristotelian doctrine that had become unchristian. I told you how he appeared again as Bacon, Lord Bacon of Verulam, who had a great influence on the spiritual life of Europe, but an influence of an essentially materialistic tendency. Moreover I told you how the counsellor of Haroun al Raschid whom I had described, appeared again as Amos Comenius. Much is said, and justly, in praise of Amos Comenius. Nevertheless, in one aspect, in his striving to introduce clear pictorial representations into the methods of teaching, he worked powerfully for materialism. For in effect, he laid the greatest stress upon the immediate perception of things with the physical senses.

Thus we see bursting in upon this earthly life at the end of the 16th and beginning of the 17th century, a stream which lies not in the straightforward line of Christian development, but which brings a foreign element, foreign to Christianity, into the spiritual and intellectual evolution of Europe. On the other hand the individualities of Aristotle and Alexander who remained united with the true stream of Michael worked on and on with all those who belonged to them. They went on working in the spiritual worlds.

Moreover other personalities were working within the same stream, partly in the spiritual worlds and partly on the earth itself. There were individualities connected with these spiritual streams and living between death and a new birth. There were others who appeared as personalities on earth in the course of the centuries. These were the individualities connected with Platonism rather than with Aristotelianism, connected also with all that the Platonic conception had since become.

Especially in the centuries following the 9th, we see Platonic spirits descending on to the earth, spirits of a Platonic trend and orientation. It was they who continued through the Middle Ages a Christian teaching regarded as heretical by official Christianity, official Catholicism, but which was nevertheless the truer Christian teaching. Meanwhile the individualities who continued the stream of Christian Aristotelianism remained, to begin with, in the spiritual worlds. For with the given conditions of civilization there was no real point of attachment for their stream down on the earth in the 9th, 10th, 11th, and 12th centuries. On the other hand, those who were more Platonic in character could un-

57

fold their spiritual life with remarkable intensity in isolated places, in isolated provinces as it were of the spirit. Interspersed with the Roman Catholic kind of Christianity which asserted itself more and more officially, we find individuals gathered in schools here and there, carrying on traditions of the ancient Mysteries and illuminating Christianity from these ancient sources. And there was one place where all these streams of old tradition seemed to flow together. I mean, of course, the School of Chartres, to which I have so often referred in recent lectures, a school which was spiritual through and through and in which there worked such great spirits as Bernardus Sylvestris, Alanus ab Insulis and others. Now what kind of a spiritual life was it which having thus evolved, flowed at length into the wonderful School of Chartres, only the external aspects of which have really become known to mankind? It was a spiritual life which has been completely silted up in modern times, a spiritual life in which the ancient traditions of the Mysteries were handed down.

Above all within that spiritual life we find a deep and spiritually penetrated conception of Nature, altogether different from that abstract conception of Nature which was afterwards made so much of, which knows only natural laws expressed in abstract thought. The spiritual stream to which I now refer received something spiritual from Nature into the human soul. So that in all Nature, not only abstract, dead, conceptual natural laws were recognised, but living creative activity. Men did not look so much to our present day chemical elements which have since commanded so much admiration, but they looked all the more deeply at what were called the Elements in the ancient sense: Earth, Water, Air and Fire. It was not a question of knowing them in words by mere tradition. The tradition was impregnated still with the most ancient of the Mysteries. And when this is so, we see in the Elements what is indeed not present in our seventy to eighty chemical elements, the world of elemental spirituality, the world of certain elemental beings into which we penetrate when we enter livingly into the four Elements.

Then we see how man himself in his outer bodily nature

58

partakes in the life and movement of the Earth, Water, Air, Fire which become in him the organic form and figure. They who thus looked into the life and movement of the Elements, of Earth, Water, Air and Fire did not see mere natural laws, but behind all this life and movement they saw a great and living Being, the Goddess Natura. And from their vision they had an immediate feeling that this Goddess Natura shows only one side of her being to man to begin with, while the other side remains hidden in the world in which man spends the time of sleep between falling asleep and re-awakening. For then the ego and astral body are in a spiritual environment which lies at the foundation of Nature. The ego and astral body are with the elemental beings who underlie the Elements. Everywhere in the scattered schools and spiritual centres to which I have referred we find the teachers speaking to larger or smaller groups of pupils, and telling them how in the outer phenomena of Nature as they appear to men in waking life, the Goddess Natura shows only one part of her living and creative being. While on the other hand, in all the working in the Elements in wind and weather, in all that surrounds the human being and constitutes him, there also works what the human being cannot see, what is hidden from him in the darkness of sleep.

These scholars of the Middle Ages felt the great Goddess Natura as the Goddess who ascends for half of the time, revealing herself in the outer movement and activity of physical sense Nature and who on the other hand descends nightly and yearly to live and work in fields of creation hidden from man by the dark consciousness of sleep.

Now this was the direct continuation of the old conception of Proserpina as it existed in the ancient Mysteries. We must consider what this signifies. We to-day have a conception of Nature woven out of abstract thought, consisting of natural laws, speaking and thinking in abstract terms, containing nothing that is alive. But in that old conception of nature they still contemplated Nature as men had once contemplated the very active Goddess Proserpina, the daughter of Demeter. And in the ideas in which the pupils of those

59

schools were instructed, proceeding as they did from a still living tradition, there were many sayings and expressions which were in reality an exact continuation of what had been said of Proserpina in the ancient Mysteries.

Then the teachers would lead the human being from a conception of his bodily life to an understanding of his life of soul. They made it clear to him: With respect to your bodily nature you consist of the Elements in which the elemental beings are working with you. But you also bear the soul within you. This is not subject to the influence of the Elements alone. On the contrary it rules over the organisation of the Elements within you and this your soul stands under the influence of the planetary world, of Mercury, Jupiter and Venus, of Sun and Moon, Saturn and Mars. Thus if psychology were to be studied, man's vision was directed upward to the secrets of the planetary world. The reality of the human being was extended from the bodily into the soul nature in such a way as to perceive always the living connection with the universe. From the working and weaving of the Elements, Earth, Water, Air and Fire, it was expanded to all that the planets do in the soul-life of man—the planets in their circling, in their glory, in the actions of their light, in their mysterious occult influences. Thus from the Goddess Natura, the successor of Proserpina, they looked up to the Intelligences, to the Genii of the planets when they wished to understand the human life of soul.

Then when it was a question of understanding the spiritual life (for the teachers of these isolated schools had not let the dogma of the 8th Council of Constantinople deter them from studying the spirit in itself)—when it was a matter of considering the spiritual life, they turned their gaze upwards to the fixed stars, and their configurations. They looked up above all to what is represented in the Zodiac. And they regarded what man bears within him as the spirit in connection with the constellations, the glory of the fixed stars, the spiritual Powers whom they knew to be there in the stars.

Thus from the whole universe, from the cosmos, they understood the human being. Thus the macrocosm was there

60

in reality, and the microcosm, man. Such was the doctrine of Nature in that time, taught with enthusiasm in isolated schools and also offered to mankind by isolated individuals who were scattered here and there. And at length as in a kind of culmination, all these things were wonderfully reproduced by such individualities as Bernardus Sylvestris, Alanus ab Insulis and others in the School of Chartres.

Wonderful indeed was this School of Chartres. If we look at its writings to-day they seem, as I already said, like catalogues of names. But in that time it was not customary to write in any other way of things which one wished to have before one in full living spirituality. One simply catalogued them as it were. He however who can read such things, he above all who can read the order in which they are placed, can very well perceive how permeated by ancient spirituality are the writings that come to us from the teachers of Chartres. But the deep spirituality of the school worked not only in the teaching that was given, nor in the fact that there were many pupils who carried out again into the world what they had learnt there. No, it also worked in a direct spiritual way. The living spirituality that was present in that School radiated out even in an occult way into the spiritual atmosphere of mankind. We see the spiritual rays of the School of Chartres passing through France even into Italy. And in many schools whose outer name has been handed down to history, a teaching about Nature was given such as I have here indicated. Brunetto Latini, the teacher of Dante, returning from his post as an Ambassador in Spain suffered at the same time a slight sunstroke and a great shock as he came near to Florence, the city of his fathers. At that moment he was really touched by the occult radiations of the School of Chartres and underwent an experience which he himself describes as follows.—He said that as he came near the city of Florence he entered a deep forest. There he first met three animals and then he met the Goddess Natura who built up the kingdoms of Nature in the very way in which this had been taught for centuries as I have indicated. He, however, beheld it directly. In the semi-pathological condition which soon passed, what had been taught in the School became immediate vision to him. Then, having seen the Goddess Natura, the successor of Proserpina, in her creative work, he beheld how man is built up out of the Elements and how the soul lives and moves in the forces of the planets. Then with his thought he was uplifted even into the heaven of the fixed stars. Thus in his own person he experienced the whole of this majestic, medieval science. And he was the teacher of Dante. Had he not been so, had he not given to his pupil Dante what he had received in this majestic vision, we should not have the Divina Commedia, for the Divina Commedia is the reflection of Brunetto Latini's teaching in the soul of Dante.

Now you must see that in that time there was no other possibility than to work with such things within the institutions of the Church, and these indeed were much freer than they afterwards became. In effect, all these teachers of Chartres belonged to Monastic Orders. We see them wearing the garment of Cistercians. We see them connected with the good tendencies within the life of the Christian Monastic Orders.

Then came a strange phase of development. During the whole of this period, when the Platonists had been active in the way just described, the Aristotelians could not work on earth. The conditions were not there. But instead, they were preparing for the Michael stream in the supersensible world, maintaining a continuous connection with those who were working on earth in the same direction and who then found their way to Chartres. The School of Chartres was in full flower from the end of the 11th and throughout the 12th century, and then a kind of supersensible exchange of ideas took place between the Platonic souls from the School of Chartres who were now coming up into the spiritual world through the gate of death and the Aristotelian souls who had remained above. It was an exchange of ideas which took place in the Middle Ages at the turn of the 12th and 13th century, as to the manner of working in the future. (Earthly terms have to be used for these things, although naturally they are not really in keeping and can easily make one appear ridiculous.)

The outcome of this exchange of ideas—since different conditions now prevailed in the spiritual life of European humanity—was that the Platonists who had been so active in Chartres and were now coming up into the supersensible world, passed on their mission to the Aristotelians. And these Aristotelian souls now descended into the physical world in order to carry forward in the way that conditions allowed, what I will call the *cosmic service of Michael.*

Within the Dominican Order, where they were active in the most manifold ways, we find again those souls who worked more in the Aristotelian sense. For the work on earth, the Platonic souls were replaced, so to speak, by the Aristotelian souls. And now there developed that system of thought which in truth can be rightly appraised to-day only within the Anthroposophical Movement—I once gave lectures here on the true form and background of Scholasticism*—there developed medieval Scholasticism, the teaching which in an age already hastening towards materialism strove to preserve as much spirituality in human concepts as it is possible to preserve.

Before Bacon of Verulam and Comenius appeared on earth, Scholasticism had been carrying forward the service of Michael. We see how Scholasticism, the so-called realistic school of philosophy, strove to rescue the source of spirituality which man bears in his thoughts. The Scholastics ascribe reality to that which man grasps through his thoughts. It is a thin, attenuated spirituality that could there be rescued, but it *is* spirituality.

Thus is the spiritual life carried forward in the evolution of the worlds. Seeing it in its reality, possessing the science of Initiation, we can do no other: we must always perceive the physical, or that which takes place in physical history upon earth, together with the spiritual that permeates it,

* *The Redemption of Thinking. A Study in the Philosophy of Thomas Aquinas.* Three lectures given by Rudolf Steiner in 1920. Translated and edited with an Introduction, Epilogue and Appendices, by A. P. Shepherd and Mildred Robertson Nicholl (Hodder & Stoughton, London, 1956).

coming from spiritual worlds. Thus we reach a united and harmonious conception. First, until the time of Chartres, the Platonic souls are working, and then the Aristotelian. We first behold the Aristotelian souls influencing with inspiration from the supersensible worlds the teachers who, as Platonic souls, are dwelling upon earth, teaching and unfolding science upon earth in earthly forms of understanding. We gaze into this living interplay; we see the teacher of Chartres sitting there on this earthly ground, unfolding his studies that are permeated by spiritual vision, while there penetrates into this earthly scene the inspiring ray from the Aristotelian soul above, bringing the Platonically coloured teachings into the right channels. It is a very different conception of life from what is usual to-day. For in external life men are so fond of contrasting and dividing Platonists from Aristotelians. But in reality it is not so. The times and epochs of the earth require teachings to be given, now in Platonic, now in Aristotelian terms. But if our wisdom includes the supersensible life in the background, we perceive the one fructifying the other, the one enclosed within the other.

Then again, when the Aristotelians were teaching in the Dominican Order, the Platonic souls, who were now once more in the spiritual world, were the inspiring genii. They had already come to an understanding in the spiritual worlds with these Aristotelian souls who afterwards descended to the earth. Life was altogether different in those times. One may believe it or not, but it was so. Looking back spiritually into those Middle Ages we find such a spirit as Alanus ab Insulis sitting in his lonely cell, given up to his studies, and receiving from the supersensible world, like a spirit-visitor who comes to him as a companion, an Aristotelian soul. Nay, even afterwards, when the Aristotelians appear in the Dominican Order, there is still a powerful consciousness of belonging to the spiritual world. We can see it in such an instance as the following. One of the Dominican teachers descends into the physical earth-life earlier than another soul with whom he is united. The other soul remains behind in the spiritual world to begin with, in order to accomplish something there which he will afterwards carry down to his companion who went before him. And at length the two are working together again on the earth. All this takes place with consciousness. In their work and activity they know themselves to be in living connection with the spiritual world.

Subsequent history has left no trace of these things. But, my dear friends, to know the truth about historical life we must not seek to derive it alone from the documents of modern time. Moreover, we must see life with open-minded vision. It may be that it unfolds in circles with which perhaps we can have little sympathy. Yet we must see it as something which is placed by karma into these very circles, and the inner significance of which is altogether different.

The task and possibility of thus reading in the real events has come to me in many remarkable ways during my life. Only now do I perceive and penetrate many an experience that I have met with in the course of my life, clear and distinct like an occult writing. Indeed for the most significant of our experiences karma works and weaves in deep and mysterious ways. And if I may say so, there is a very strong karma underlying the fact that to-day and in recent times, at many places, I have been speaking of such things as the School of Chartres, and what preceded and what came after it. For the greatest of those who taught in the School of Chartres belonged to the Cistercian Order. Now the Cistercian Order, like the other Orders in the Catholic stream of development, has become decadent, but in this growing decadence there is also much illusion of appearance. For individualities occasionally find themselves in outer life-connections to which they do not properly belong, while in reality they are carrying forward old threads of spiritual life which are indeed of the greatest value for Anthroposophy itself. But life and karma brings them into these outer connections. Thus I have always been struck by the fact that from my earliest youth, until a certain period of life, something of the Cistercian Order again and again approached me. Having gone through the elementary school, I narrowly escaped—for reasons which I explained in my autobiography, *The Story of my Life*—becoming a pupil in a *gymnasium* or grammar school conducted by the Cistercian Order. Everything seemed to be leading in this direction; but my parents, as I have explained, eventually decided to send me to the modern school instead. Thus I did not become a pupil in the grammar school connected with the Cistercians, and, needless to say, this was also for very good karmic reasons.

But the modern school which I attended was only five steps away from the Cistercian grammar school. Thus we made the acquaintance of all those excellent Cistercian teachers whose work was indeed of a high quality at that time. I need not speak of the Order itself; it is the individuals to whom I refer. To this day I think with profound appreciation of one of those Cistercian priests who taught German literature at that grammar school with deep enthusiasm. And I see the Cistercian priest before me in many other individualities, in the Alleegasse in Wiener Neustadt, where the teachers used to walk up and down before the school hours began— Cistercian priests in civilian costume, eminently gifted men. At that time I was far more concerned to read the essays of the teachers in the school year-book at the end of the year, than the ordinary text-books during the year. I read with keen devotion what these Cistercians wrote of their own wisdom in the year-book of the grammar school in Wiener Neustadt.

In short, the Cistercian Order was near to me. And without a doubt (though these of course are hypotheses such as one uses only for purposes of illustration), if I had gone to the Cistercian school I should, as a matter of course, have become a Cistercian.

Then I came to Vienna. (All these things are described in *The Story of my Life*.) After a time I came into the circle around Marie Eugenie delle Grazie, where many professors of the theological faculty in Vienna used to gather. I learned to know some of them intimately. All those professors were members of the Cistercian Order. Thus once again I came together with Cistercians, and through the currents which flow through the Cistercian Order to-day, I have been able to follow many things back into the past.

To show how karma works I will refer to one event. I had to give a lecture. Now through the afternoon teas at delle Grazie's I had grown well acquainted with the Cistercian professors of theology who frequented her house. I gave a lecture. A priest of the Cistercian Order was there—a remarkable and excellent man. When I had finished my lecture he made a very peculiar remark, the nature of which I will only indicate by saying: he uttered words in which was contained his memory of having been together with me in a former life on earth.

Such things do indeed educate us for life. It was in the year 1889. In *Das Goetheanum,** of course, I could only take the external aspect of these things; but my autobiographical essays will be published as a book with added notes in which the inner aspect will also be duly dealt with. Here, you see, I have told you something of the karmic foundations which have made it possible for me to speak at all in this form about these particular spiritual streams. For one cannot study these things by mere study. One's study of them must consist in life itself.

Thus I have shown how the Platonic stream and the Aristotelian worked together. Then the Aristotelians too went once more through the gate of death. And as we know, with the age of the Spiritual Soul, materialism became more and more predominant on earth. But at the very time when materialism took its start on earth there was founded in the supersensible worlds a kind of Michael School. As I said, we can refer to these things only with our everyday terminology. It was a far-spread School of Michael in which spirits

* The weekly periodical published at the Goetheanum, Dornach, Switzerland. Rudolf Steiner died before the autobiographical essays had been completed, but those that were available have been collected in the book *Rudolf Steiner, An Autobiography*, 2nd Edition 1980, published by Multimedia Publishing Corp., New York.

like Bernardus Sylvestris and Alanus ab Insulis were united after death. And with them once more Alexander and Aristotle. These and other human souls who were not in earthly incarnation at that time, were united here with spiritual beings who, though they spend their lives without ever being incarnated on the earth, are yet connected with earthly souls. Michael himself was a Teacher, gazing back over all that had been the great teachings of the ancient Mysteries, comprehending in a marvellous sweep of vision the secrets of the ancient Mysteries, and opening out at the same time a mighty panorama of what was to come.

In one form or another we find certain souls who took part in that supersensible school in the 14th/15th century. They had more or less been connected together in many lives on earth. We find them among the hosts which strive towards the stream of Michael, receiving into the impulses of their will what we may call: The will to be united with the stream of Michael.

We gaze upon these souls. Very few of them were on earth. Most of them were in the life between death and a new birth, partaking in that supersensible gathering, in that spiritual school. We find them there, these souls, we find them there, harkening to the teachings of Michael, and we find them again to-day in the souls who, connected on the earth, unfold a sincere and upright striving of their inner life towards the Anthroposophical Movement.

In the karma of those who tend with inner sincerity towards the Anthroposophical Movement, there lie the deep impulses, the karmic significance of which must again be studied in the spiritual worlds themselves. Of course the fact that those souls were driven by their karma to such a heavenly community at that time, is due again to the fact that in former earthly lives they had shaped their karma accordingly, so that it led them there. Nevertheless one cannot recognise the karma of human souls without looking, not only at what happens at any given time on earth, but also at what happens between death and a new birth.

Our outlook on the world is infinitely enriched by this.

Contemplating the souls who labour in the world—and in the last resort this applies to all men—we no longer have to begin at the point where they enter earthly existence, or cease at the point where they die; for in effect they neither then begin to work, nor do they cease. And in all that takes place spiritually, not only the souls that are incarnated on the earth to-day are working, but other souls, who are now between death and a new birth, and who send their rays of influence in upon the earth. In our own actions their impulses are contained. For all these things work together, even as the deeds on earth penetrate into the heavenly regions, and continue working there, as I indicated pictorially, for instance, in the characters of Capesius and Strader in the first Mystery Play.

Brunetto Latini, Dante's teacher, he is there. He died. He went through the gate of death, but death itself is a transformation of life. He is still there. He works on, and we find him if we seek him spiritually.

The picture of the spiritual evolution of mankind is made complete if we are able to include the so-called dead. Nay, in reality, they are far more living than the so-called living. In very many things that happen on the earth we find Brunetto Latini living and working to-day, although he is not incarnate on the earth. Thus you will see how intimately united the earthly life is with the supersensible. We cannot speak at all of a supersensible world separated from the earthly world of sense. For everything that is of the senses is permeated at the same time supersensibly, and everything that is supersensible is revealed somewhere and somewhen in the world of sense. Moreover we can only truly receive and understand the earthly life if we recognise that these things are behind it.

This, my dear friends, is to be the future of the Anthroposophical Movement since the Christmas Foundation Meeting. We must treat of the supersensible facts openly and without reserve, confessing them in fullness of knowledge. This should be the esoteric trait permeating the Anthroposophical Movement. Thus alone will it be possible to give it its real spiritual content.

For you see, all that I described to you as the stream of Michael has gone on into our time. But individualities appearing again on earth have to make use, in the first place, of the physical bodies that are possible in a given age. They must find their way into the impulses of education which a given age provides. In the materialistic age all these things become their external garment. And our materialistic age offers the greatest imaginable hindrances to souls who had a rich spirituality in former lives on earth. To pour this spirituality into the bodies of this age, especially when they have to be prepared by modern educational methods, is extraordinarily difficult. Thus you need not wonder when I say: The souls which strive earnestly towards Anthroposophy are to be found in this way in former epochs of evolution. We cannot lay the foundations of true knowledge unless we can perceive the real interplay of all that lives and works in the world. For spiritual research itself depends on the spiritual life and requires us to seek the spiritual along its own true path. The paths of the spirit are different in every age. In our age they are possible only if we have beneath our feet the firm ground of a spiritual knowledge of external Nature.

The former age which I described within the stream of Michael was followed by one which here on the earth shows an altogether materialistic aspect, an age in which all things are developed materialistically. In the supersensible evolution of this age there is the most intensive work of preparation for the impulses of Michael, which have now been carried down, so to speak, from heaven to the earth. But this new age to-day cannot take its start from what has gone before in the last few centuries. We must indeed be familiar with the things that have unfolded upon earth in the last few centuries, but we cannot take our start from them. With the consciousness of this modern age we must take our start from what has taken place in the supersensible during the last few centuries. In saying this we touch upon ground which must become the basis of anthroposophical life and work in this present time. Conceptions such as I have explained in the last few lectures must not merely be received with cold intellect and indifferent hearts. They must be received by the full human being, by the whole compass of the human heart and mind. Anthroposophy can mean something for mankind only if it is received with the whole compass of the human heart and soul.

Such is the foundation of the will of the Anthroposophical Movement, which is united since the Foundation Meeting with the Anthroposophical Society. We long that this should enter deeply into the souls of human beings who are united with this Movement, that they should grow conscious of what is truly connected with their karma in the depths of their own souls.

Thus we have laid a kind of foundation, and from this point we will proceed next Sunday when we will study the further course of the stream of Michael, so as to perceive its resulting tasks for Anthroposophy and for the whole spiritual life of the present time.

Lecture 5

Having spoken so often about the School of Chartres and its great significance for the inner spiritual life of the West, I have received a welcome gift during the last few days: a gift of pictures, some of which have been put up here for you to see. Others will be added next Tuesday. In these pictures you will see what wonderful architectural works and works of sculpture in the mediaeval sense, arose at the place where flourished that spiritual life of which I have now spoken so often.

The personalities who were gathered in the School of Chartres still had the impulse, even in the 12th century, to enter as teachers or students into the living spiritual life that had arisen in the turning-point of time—I mean in the epoch of European evolution when humanity, inasmuch as they were seekers after knowledge, still sought it in the living weaving and working of the nature-beings, and not in the conception of void and abstract natural laws.

Thus in the School of Chartres there was a deep devotion to spiritual powers, notably to those that hold sway in Nature. All this was cultivated there—no longer, it is true, by Initiates into the ancient Mysteries—but by personalities who had the heart and mind to receive from tradition much that had once been direct spiritual experience. And I have told you of the mysterious radiations of light from the School of Chartres which we can truly recognise in the spirit of Brunetto Latini, the great teacher of Dante. I tried to explain how the individualities of Chartres worked on in the spiritual worlds in unison with those who afterwards came down, more in the Dominican Order, as the bearers of Scholasticism. We may put it thus.—The individualities of Chartres were obliged to see, out of the signs of the times, that there would be no place for them within the earthly life until the time when the

73

element of Michael, which was to begin at the end of the 19th century, should have been working for a while on earth.

In a far-reaching sense these individualities of Chartres took part in the supersensible teachings of which I spoke last time—teachings that were given under the aegis of Michael himself, so as to pour forth impulses which were to hold good for the spiritual life of coming centuries. And it may be said indeed that anyone who would devote himself to the cultivation of spiritual life to-day must necessarily stand under the influence of those great impulses.

Broadly speaking we may say that there have been very few reincarnations of the spirits of Chartres hitherto. Nevertheless it was granted to me to look back upon the School of Chartres through a certain stimulus, if I may describe it so, which came to me out of the life of the present time.

There was a monk in the School of Chartres who was altogether devoted to the life-element that existed in that school. But in the School of Chartres, especially if one was truly devoted to it, one felt as it were a twilight mood of the spiritual life. All that was reminiscent still of the great and deep impulses of the spiritual Platonism that had been handed down—all this was living in Chartres. But it lived in such a way that the bearers of the spiritual life of Chartres said to themselves: In the future, alas, the civilisation of Europe will no longer be receptive for this living, Platonic spirituality.

It is touching to see how the School of Chartres preserves as it were the portraits of the inspiring genii of the Seven Liberal Arts, as they were called: Grammatica, Dialectica, Rhetorica, Arithmetica, Geometria, Astronomia and Musica. Even in the reception of the Spiritual that was contained in the Seven Liberal Arts, they still saw in them the living gifts of the gods, coming to man through spiritual beings. They did not see the mere communication of dead thoughts about dead laws of Nature. And they could see that Europe in the future would no longer be receptive to these things. Hence there was a feeling of evening twilight in the spiritual life.

Now one of those monks who was especially devoted to the

74

teachings and the works of Chartres, was, after all, reincarnated in our time. He was reincarnated, moreover, in such a way that one could find in this case most wonderfully the echo and reflection of the former life in the present. This personality lived in our time as an authoress who was not only my acquaintance, but my friend.* She died a considerable time ago. She bore within her a strange mood of soul, about which I should not have spoken until now, although I observed it many years ago. To speak of these things has indeed only been possible since the Christmas feeling came over our Anthroposophical Society. For this has brought a peculiar illumination over these things, and it is possible, as I have already said, to speak about such matters openly and without embarrassment to-day.

When one was in conversation with that authoress, she returned again and again to the theme that she would like to die. But her desire to die did not spring from a sentimental or hypochondriac, nay, not even from a melancholic mood of soul. If one had the psychological vision to enter into such things, one found one's way far, far back into her soul until at length one had to say: It is the echo and reflection of a former life on earth. In a former life on earth a seed was planted which now comes forth, I will not say in the longing for death, but in this feeling that the soul, being now incarnated, yet has nothing really to do with this present age.

Her writings, too, are of this nature. They seem to be written out of a different world—not indeed as to their facts and communications—but as to their mood and feeling. And we can understand this mood only if we find the way from the dim light of her writings, from the dim light that lived as a fundamental disposition in her own soul, back to that monk of Chartres who felt in Chartres the evening twilight mood of a living Platonism.

In this authoress it was not a question of temperament or melancholy or sentimentality; it was the raying-in of a former life on earth. And her present soul was like a mirror into which the life of Chartres really penetrated. Not indeed the

* Elisabeth Glück (Betty Paoli), poetess and writer, 1814–1894.

content of the teachings of Chartres, but their moods and feelings, had been transmitted from the one life to the other in this personality. Transplanting oneself into these moods, and looking back, one could receive in them as it were spiritual photographs of the personalities who are also to be found by direct spiritual research in the worlds where they now are—the personalities who taught in Chartres.

Thus you see, life brings to one in many ways the karmic possibilities to gaze into these matters. Last time, I described my experiences with the Cistercian Order. To-day I would supplement what I then said by referring to the evening twilight mood of the School of Chartres which penetrated into the heart and soul of an extraordinarily interesting personality, who lived again in the present time. She has long ago found her way back into the worlds for which she longed. She has found her way back to the Fathers of Chartres. And if her whole soul-life had not been dominated by a kind of weariness as the karmic outcome of the mood-of-soul of yonder monk of Chartres, I could scarcely imagine a personality more fitted to behold the spiritual life of the present day in connection with the traditional life of the Middle Ages.

There is another thing which I would mention here. When there are such karmic impulses working deep in the foundations of the soul, we find what is otherwise a very rare occurrence: we find in the physical expression of the countenance in a later incarnation, a likeness to the former. The face of yonder monk and of the authoress of the present time were indeed extraordinarily alike.

Now in these connections I will gradually pass on to the karma of the Anthroposophical Society, or of the individualities of its members. For as I said last time, a large number of the souls who stand sincerely within the Anthroposophical Movement were connected somewhere and somewhen with that stream of Michael which I must now characterise. You will remember all that I have said in this connection about Alexander and Aristotle and about the events in supersensible worlds at the time when the 8th Council in Constantinople

76

took place here in this world of sense. You will remember what I said of the continuation, in the spiritual and in the physical, of the life of the Court of Haroun al Raschid, until at length I spoke of that supersensible School which stood under the aegis of Michael himself. Deeply significant was the teaching of that School. On the one hand it pointed again and again to the connections with the ancient Mysteries, to all that must now come forth once more in a new form from the content of the ancient Mysteries, to permeate modern civilisation with spirituality. On the other hand it pointed to the impulses which souls, devoted to the spiritual life, must have for their work into the future. And we know that from an understanding of the spiritual stream we may also come to understand how Anthroposophy, in its real essence, signifies the impulse for a renewal, for a true and sincere understanding of the Christ-Impulse.

For in the Anthroposophical Movement we find two kinds of souls. A large number of them have partaken in those currents which were, so to speak, the officially Christian ones in the first centuries. They witnessed all that came into the world as Christianity, notably in the times of Constantine, and immediately after him. Many of those who approached Christianity with the very deepest sincerity at that time and received it with inner depth and penetration, many of them are found in the Anthroposophical Society to-day with the deep impulse towards an understanding of Christianity. I do not mean so much the Christians who followed such movements as that of Constantine himself; I rather mean those Christians who claimed to be the true Christians, who were distributed in different Christian sects. In those Christian sects we find many of the souls who to-day approach the Anthroposophical Movement sincerely, though often through subconscious impulses which the surface consciousness may even largely misinterpret.

But there are other souls: there are those who did not partake directly in that development of Christianity. They either partook in Christianity at a later stage of its development when the deep inner life of the sects was no longer

77

there, or on the other hand—and this is the most important—
they still had, living and unextinguished in the depths of their
souls, much of what was experienced in pre-Christian time as
the ancient wisdom of the heathen Mysteries. They too often
partook in Christianity; but it did not make so deep an impression upon them as upon the other souls described before.
For there still remained alive in them the impression of the
teachings, the rituals and practices of ancient Mysteries. Now
among those who have entered the Anthroposophical Movement in this way we find many who are seeking for the Christ
in an abstract sense. The other souls above described are
happy, so to speak, to find Christianity once more within the
Anthroposophical Movement. But many of the souls I now
mean grasp with real inner understanding the Cosmic
Christianity which Anthroposophy contains. Christ as the
Cosmic Spirit of the Sun is taken hold of most especially by
the souls (and they are very numerous in the Anthroposophical Movement) in the depths of whom much is still living
of what they underwent in connection with ancient heathen
Mysteries.

Now all this is deeply connected with the currents of the
whole spiritual life of mankind in the present time—I mean
the present time in a wider sense, reaching over decades and
centuries.

Anthroposophy after all has grown out of the spiritual
life of the present time, and though in its contents it has
nothing directly in common with this spiritual life, karmically
it has grown out of it in many ways. We must turn our eyes
to many things which do not apparently belong to what
works in Anthroposophy directly, if we would include in our
spiritual horizon all that partook in the different streams I
have mentioned. I said a little while ago that we only truly
understand what takes place outwardly on the physical plane
if we see in the background what is poured down from the
fields of the spirit into these events as they take place on the
physical plane. We must regain the courage to bring into our
present life that feeling of the ancient Mysteries. We must
connect the physical events not merely abstractly with a

vaguely Pantheistic or Theistic or whatever spiritual life. We must become able to trace the detailed events, nay more, the inner experiences of men within these events, to the spiritual source and background.

We are led to do so among other things by something that belongs to the deepest tasks of the present time. For in the present time we must seek again for a real knowledge of man in body, soul and spirit—not a knowledge rooted in abstract ideas or laws, but one that is able to look into the true foundation of the human being as a whole. To gain such knowledge man must be searched through and through in his conditions of health and sickness; and not in a merely physical sense as is customary to-day, for then we should not learn to know the human being. By merely physical knowledge we can never learn to know what works so deeply into the life of man, determining his destiny: his unhappiness, his sickness, his abilities or absence of abilities. Karma in all its forms—this we can only know if from the starting-point of the physical we can trace the spiritual life of a man and his inner life of soul.

How do people work, in the ordinary scientific striving of to-day ? They study the human being quite externally as to his organs and vessels, his nerves, the vessels of the circulation of the blood and so forth. But when the health and sickness of man are studied in this fashion one cannot find the spirit and soul in all these things.

Indeed the anatomist or physiologist of to-day may well speak in the words of a famous astronomer of the past, who, in answer to a question which his sovereign had put to him, replied: " I have searched through the whole universe, through all the stars and all their movements, but I have found no God ! " So said the astronomer. And the anatomist or physiologist of to-day could say: " I have searched through them all—heart and kidneys, stomach and brain, blood-vessels and nerves—but I have found neither soul nor spirit."

All the problems and difficulties of modern medicine, for example, are subject to this influence. And all these things must be dealt with in the Anthroposophical Movement to-day, according to the tasks which are placed before it. In general terms these questions must be unfolded before the Anthroposophical Society as a whole; in detail they must be treated in an expert way within the several groups. Thus, for example, I am now speaking on Pastoral Medicine to a group who are prepared for it by training and profession. Here we must seek the way into those great connections which proceed in the last resort from the workings of the streams of karma. In time to come it will be seen how pathology and therapeutics, how the observation of man in sickness and disease, will make it absolutely necessary to enter into the deep questions of the soul and spirit. As I have said again and again, the external and physical—the physical as presented by natural science—is to be respected in the fullest sense. Yet men will find themselves compelled to take into account the higher members of man's nature when considering disease and health. This will be seen in the book* on which my dear fellow-worker Frau Dr. Wegman and I are working together, on the subject of man in health and in disease. Now these researches especially, seeking the ways of entry from the physical man into the spiritual, can only lead to good and promising results if we set about them in the right way. For in such work we must not only use the knowledge-forces of the present, but we must use the knowledge-forces which arise by picking up the threads of karma—the karmic threads proceeding from the history and evolution of mankind. We must indeed work with the forces of karma in order to penetrate these secrets.

In the first volume, only the beginnings of our work will be published. The work will then be carried forward and from the more elementary expositions we shall proceed to unfold the particular knowledge of man which can arise from this medical, therapeutic and pathological aspect of spiritual science. This work has only been made possible through the

* *Fundamentals of Therapy; an Extension of the Art of Healing through Spiritual Knowledge*, by Rudolf Steiner, Ph.D. and Ita Wegman, M.D. (Zürich). English translation by George Adams, M.A., published by Rudolf Steiner Press, London.

presence in Frau Dr. Wegman of a personality whose medical studies have entered into her in such a way as to evolve quite naturally, as a matter of course, towards a spiritual conception and perception of the human being.

Now it is in the course of these researches, when we behold in spiritual perspective all the workings of the human organs, that those perceptions also arise which lead us in turn to the deeper karmic connections. The same manner of perception must be evolved to perceive the spiritual realities that underlie, not the whole man, but his several organs. (For, if you will, it is the Jupiter world that underlies one organ, the Venus world that underlies another, and so forth.) The same insight which we must evolve in this direction, leads also to the possibility of perceiving human personalities in past earthly lives. For in the present earthly life man stands before us within the limits of his skin. But when we become able to gaze into his single organs, what was contained within the skin expands and expands. Each of the single organs points us to a different direction of the universe. The organs prepare the roads that lead us far out into the macrocosm, until far out yonder the human being once again appears as a complete and rounded whole. It is the human being built up once more in the spirit, having transcended the present form, the form that is enclosed within the skin—it is this that we need. For the sum-total of the human organs—which even physically is altogether different from what the present-day anatomist or physiologist conceives—when we trace it out into the cosmos, leads to perceptions which correspond in turn to the spiritual perception of the former earthly lives of man. Then we experience the inner connections that shed their light upon the evolution and history of mankind, explaining what is physically there to-day. For in reality the whole past of human beings lives in the present time. Yet the vague and abstract saying by itself is of no avail. Materialists too will say the same. The point is to perceive *how* the past is living in the present.

And of this I would now give you an example, an example which is in itself so wonderful that it called forth in me the greatest imaginable wonder when I first came to it as a result of spiritual research. And many things which I have said before must now be rectified, or at any rate must be completed, by that which I shall now set forth.

You see, for one who studies history with feeling for its inner meaning, a certain event in the first centuries of Christianity is wrapped in the atmosphere of a strange mystery. We see on the one side a personality of whom we may well think that in his inner life he was little fitted to take hold of Christianity or to make it what it then became, the official Christianity of the West. I mean the Emperor Constantine, of whom we have so often spoken. Then, side by side with him (not literally of course, but gazing back into that age from a considerable distance in time), side by side with Constantine we see *Julian the Apostate*. Julian the Apostate, he of a truth was one in whom the wisdom of the Mysteries was living, as we may know. Julian the Apostate could speak of a Threefold Sun. Indeed he lost his life through being regarded as a betrayer of the Mysteries, because he spoke about the Threefold Sun. Of these things it was no longer allowed to speak in his time; still less would it have been allowed in earlier times. But Julian the Apostate stood in a peculiar relation to Christianity. In a certain sense we must again and again be surprised that the genius, the fine spirituality and intellect of Julian was so little receptive to the greatness of Christianity. It was simply due to the fact that in his environment he saw very little of what he conceived as a true inner sincerity, whereas among those who introduced him to the ancient Mysteries he found great sincerity—positive, active sincerity. Such was the case with Julian the Apostate.

Yonder in Asia he was murdered. Many a fable is told about the murder. The truth is that it took place because he was regarded as a betrayer of the Mysteries. It was a murder altogether pre-arranged.

Now if we make ourselves to some extent acquainted with that which lived in Julian we cannot but be deeply interested in the question: How did his individuality live on in later

82

times ? For his was a peculiar individuality, one of whom it must be said that he would have been better fitted than Constantine, better than Clodvig and all the others, to make straight the ways of Christianity. This lay inherent in his soul. If the time had been favourable, if the conditions had existed, he could have brought about out of the ancient Mysteries a straightforward continuation from the pre-Christian Christ, the true macrocosmic Logos, to the Christ who was to work on within mankind after the Mystery of Golgotha. He was indeed a vessel well prepared. Strange as it may sound, we find it so, if we enter into his true spirit. We find in the foundations of his soul the true impulse to take hold of Christianity. But he did not let it emerge, he suppressed it, misled by the stupidities which Celsus had written about Jesus. It does indeed happen now and then that men of real genius are led astray by the stupidest effusions of their fellow-men. Thus we may have the feeling: Julian would really have been the soul to make straight the ways of Christianity and to bring Christianity into its true and proper channel.

We now leave the soul of Julian the Apostate in that earthly life and follow the same individuality with the highest interest through spiritual worlds. But there is always something vague and unclear about it. Only the most intense spiritual striving can come at length to a clear perception of his further course.

On many matters very adequate ideas existed in the Middle Ages. They might be legendary, but they were adequate; they corresponded to the real events. Legendary though they may be, how adequate are the narratives that centred round the personality of Alexander the Great. How vividly his life appears, as I already said, in the description of Lamprecht the Priest !

But that which lives on of Julian, lives on in such a way that we must say again and again: It seeks to disappear from before the vision of mankind. And as we seek to follow it we have the greatest difficulty, so to speak, in keeping it within our spiritual field of vision. Again and again it escapes us. We trace it through the centuries into the Middle Ages and it escapes us. But when at length we do succeed in following it to the end, we land at a strange place, which though it be not historic in the proper sense, is in reality more than historic. We come at length to the figure of a woman, in whom we find again the soul of Julian the Apostate. It was a woman who accomplished an important deed in her life under the impression of an essentially painful event. For she beheld, not in herself, but in the person of another, an image of the fate of Julian the Apostate, inasmuch as Julian the Apostate went on a campaign to the East and there lost his life by treachery.

The woman whom I mean is *Herzeleide*, the mother of Parsifal, who was an historic character though history itself tells nothing of her. In Gamuret, whom she married and who lost his life through treachery upon an Eastern campaign, she was pointed to her own destiny in the former life as Julian the Apostate. This went deep into her soul, and under this impression she achieved what is told to us in a legendary way —yet it is historic in the truest sense—of the education of Parsifal by Herzeleide.

The soul of Julian the Apostate who had remained thus in the depths and of whom one would believe that it should have been his very mission to prepare the right way for Christianity—this soul is found again in the Middle Ages in the body of a woman who sent out Parsifal, to seek and to find the esoteric paths for Christianity.

Mysterious like this, and full of riddles, are the paths of mankind in the background, in the foundations of existence. This example—and it is strangely interwoven with the one which I already told you in connection with the School of Chartres—this example may make you realise how wonderful are the paths of the human soul and the paths of evolution for all mankind.

We shall continue speaking of it in the next lecture, when I shall have more to say of the life of Herzeleide and of what was then sent forth, physically, in Parsifal. I shall begin next time at this point where we must break off to-day.

Lecture 6

To-day I wish to continue with the subject I placed before you the day before yesterday. We were tracing the thread of evolution which enters into the spiritual life of the present time, and we left off with the individuality of Julian the Apostate. I told you that this individuality was next incarnated in one who is only known by legendary accounts, whose secret is contained in the Parsifal legend, in the name of Herzeleide. In this life as Herzeleide, the soul of Julian the Apostate entered into a far deeper inner life. The soul-life of the individuality was deepened, as was indeed necessary after the many storms and inner moods of opposition which he had undergone in his life as Julian the Apostate.

But this later life of which I told you—this life as Herzeleide —spread itself out over the former life as Julian the Apostate like a warm embalming cloud. Thus the soul grew more intense and deep and inward, and grew richer, too, in manifold impulses of the inner life.

Now this soul was among those who had carried over something of the ancient Mysteries. Julian had lived within the substance of the ancient Mysteries at a time when their light was still radiant in many ways. Thus he had received into himself much spirituality of the cosmos. All this had been as it were pressed back during the incarnation as Herzeleide; but it was none the less pressing forth in the soul, and thus we find the same individuality again in the 16th century; we find arising in him once more, in a Christianised form, what he had undergone as Julian the Apostate. For the same individuality reappears in the 16th century as *Tycho de Brahe*, and stands face to face with the Copernican world-conception which emerges within Western civilisation at that time.

The Copernican world-conception pictures the universe in

a way, which if followed to its logical conclusions would tend to drive all spirituality out of the cosmos in man's conception of it. The Copernican world-picture leads at length to a mechanical, machine-like conception of the universe in space. It was after all in view of this Copernican picture of the world that the famous astronomer said to Napoleon: he had searched through all the universe and he could find no God. It is, indeed, an entire elimination of spirituality.

The individuality of whom I am now speakng, who had now returned as Tycho de Brahe, could not submit to this. Thus we see Tycho de Brahe accepting in his world-conception what is useful of Copernicanism, but rejecting the absolute movement of the earth ascribed to it according to the Copernican world-picture. In Tycho de Brahe we see these things united with true spirituality. When we consider the course of his life, it is indeed evident how a karma from ancient time is pressing its way forth with might and main into this life as Tycho de Brahe, seeking to enter the substance of his consciousness. Such is his spirituality. We remember how his Danish relatives sought to hold him fast at all costs in the profession of a lawyer, and we see how, living as a tutor, he steals the hours by night in which to commune with the gods. And here an extraordinary thing appears. All this is contained in his biography. We shall see presently how deeply significant it is for a true estimate of this individuality of Tycho de Brahe—Julian—Herzeleide. With the most primitive instruments contrived and manufactured by himself, he discovers considerable errors in calculation which had entered into the determination of the orbits of Saturn and Jupiter. We have this remarkable scene in the life of Tycho de Brahe. As a young man with the most primitive instruments with which other people would not dream of trying to accomplish anything, he feels impelled one day to seek the exact places of Saturn and Jupiter in the heavens. In his case all these things are strongly permeated with spiritual content. And this spiritual content leads him to a conception of the universe such as we must have if we are striving once again to the modern science of Initiation, when at length we come to

86

speak of spiritual beings as we speak of physical men on earth. For in reality we can ever meet them, and there is in fact only a difference in quality of being as between those individualities who are now on the physical plane and those who are discarnate, living between death and a new birth.

These things kindled in Tycho de Brahe an extraordinarily deep and penetrating vision of spiritual connections. I mean the connections which appear when we no longer regard everything on earth as though it were caused by earthly impulses alone, and on the other hand consider the stars only in mathematical calculations, but when we perceive the interplay of impulses from the stars with the historic impulses within mankind. In Tycho de Brahe's soul there lived instinctively what he had brought with him from his life as Julian the Apostate. In that former life it had not been permeated with rationalism or intellectualism. It had been intuitive, imaginative—for such was the inner life of Julian the Apostate. With all this he succeeded in doing something that made a great sensation.

He could make little impression on his contemporaries with his astronomic opinions, differing as they did from Copernicus, or with his other astronomical achievements. He observed countless stars and made a map of the heavens which alone made it possible for Kepler afterwards to reach his great results. For it was on the basis of Tycho de Brahe's mapping of the stars that Kepler discovered his famous laws. But none of these things could have made so great an impression on his contemporaries as a discovery relatively unimportant in itself, but very striking. He foretold almost to the day the death of the Sultan Soliman, which afterwards occurred as he had foretold it. Here we see ancient perceptions working into a later time in a spiritual intellectuality. Perceptions which Julian the Apostate had received light up again in modern time in Tycho de Brahe. Tycho de Brahe is indeed one of the most interesting of human souls. In the 17th century he passed on th.ough the gate of death and entered the spiritual world. Now in the spiritual currents which I have described as those of Michael, this being, Tycho de Brahe—Julian the Apostate—Herzeleide, constantly emerges. In one or another of the supersensible functions he is in fact always there. Hence too we find him in those great events in the supersensible world at the end of the 18th and beginning of the 19th century which are connected with this stream of Michael.

I told you already of the great supersensible School of instruction in the 15th, 16th centuries which stood under the aegis of Michael himself. Then there began for those who had been within this School a life which took its course in such a way that activities and forces unfolded in the spiritual world worked down into the physical, worked in connection with the physical world. For example, in the time that immediately followed the period of the supersensible School of Michael, an important task was allotted to an individuality of whose continued life I have often spoken—I mean the individuality of Alexander the Great.

I have already spoken, here at Dornach too, of Lord Bacon of Verulam as the reincarnated Haroun al Raschid. We know how intense and determining an influence Bacon's conceptions had on the whole succeeding evolution of the spiritual life, notably in its finer impulses and movements. Now the remarkable thing is this, that in Lord Bacon himself something took place which we may describe as a morbid elimination of old spirituality. For such spirituality he had after all possessed when he was Haroun al Raschid.

And thus we see, proceeding from the impulse of Lord Bacon, a whole world of 'daemonic beings. The world was literally filled supersensibly and sensibly with daemonic beings. (When I say " sensibly " I mean *not* of course, visibly, but within the world of sense.)

Now it chiefly fell to the individuality of Alexander to wage war against these daemonic idols of Lord Bacon, Francis Bacon of Verulam. And similar activities, exceedingly important ones, were taking place on earth below. For otherwise the materialism of the 19th century would have broken in upon the world in a far more devastating way even than it did. Similar activities, taking place in the spiritual and in the physical world together, were allotted to the stream of Michael, until at length at the end of the 18th and the beginning of the 19th century there took place in supersensible regions what I have already described as the enactment of a great and sublime supersensible ritual and ceremony.

In the supersensible world at that time a cult was instituted and enacted in real imaginations of a spiritual kind. Thus we may say: At the end of the 18th and beginning of the 19th century there hovers in the immediate neighbourhood of the physical world of sense a great supersensible event, consisting in supersensible acts of ritual, an unfolding of mighty pictures of the spiritual life of beings of the universe, the Beings of the Hierarchies in connection with the great ether-workings of the universe and the human workings upon earth. I say " in the immediate neighbourhood," meaning of course, adjoining this physical world in a qualitative, not in a *spatial* sense. It is interesting to see how at a most favourable moment a little miniature picture of this supersensible cult and action flowed into Goethe's spirit. Transformed and changed and in miniature we have this picture set down by Goethe in his fairy story of the Green Snake and the Beautiful Lily. . . .

There was, then, a great supersensible action in which those above all took part who had partaken in the stream of Michael, in all the revelations supersensible and sensible, of which I told you. Now here again and again the individuality who was last present upon earth in Tycho de Brahe, plays a very great part. And it was his constant striving to preserve the great and lasting impulses of what we call paganism, of the old life of the Mysteries. It was his striving to preserve it in effect towards a better understanding of Christianity. He had entered Christianity when he lived as the soul of Herzeleide. Now it was his striving to introduce into the Christian conception all that he had received through his Initiation as Julian the Apostate. For it was this especially which seemed so important to the souls of whom I have spoken. The many souls who are now to be found in the Anthroposophical Movement or strive towards this Movement with sincerity are united with all these spiritual streams. By its very essence and nature they feel themselves attracted by the School of Michael, and Tycho de Brahe had a great influence in this. At the end of the 19th and beginning of the 20th century, especially at the end of the 19th century, these souls have descended to the earth, prepared not only to feel the Christ as He is felt in the various Confessions, but to feel Him and behold Him as the Cosmic Christ in His universal majesty and glory. The souls were prepared for this even supersensibly, between death and the new birth. They were prepared by such influences as that of Tycho de Brahe, of the soul who was last incarnated in Tycho de Brahe.

This individuality therefore played an extraordinarily important part continuously within the stream of Michael.

You see, the souls were constantly looking towards the approaching dominion of Michael. They were looking towards it in the old supersensible School of the 15th and16th centuries, and they were looking towards it again during the enactment of that supersensible ceremony which was to introduce and, as it were, to consecrate from the spiritual worlds the subsequent Michael dominion upon earth. Now as I have already indicated, a large number of Platonically gifted souls have remained in the spiritual worlds since the time they worked in Chartres. (I have placed here for your inspection to-day other pictures of the series from Chartres which I received. They are pictures of the Prophets and also of the wonderful architecture of Chartres.) The individualities of the teachers of Chartres, who were of a Platonic tendency, remained in the spiritual world. It was more the Aristotelians who descended to the earth, finding their way largely into the Dominican Order. Then, after a certain time, they united again with the Platonists in the spiritual world and went on working together with them supersensibly, from the spiritual world. Thus we may say: the souls of Platonic character have remained behind. They have not appeared again on earth, not at any rate the more important individualities among them. They are waiting till the end of this century. But on the other hand, many who felt themselves drawn to what I have described as the Michael deeds in the supersensible, have come down and entered the stream of the Anthroposophical Movement inasmuch as they have felt sincerely drawn on earth to such a spiritual Movement.

We may say in truth: what lives in Anthroposophy was kindled first by the Michael School of instruction in the 15th, 16th centuries, and by the great religious act that took place in the supersensible at the end of the 18th and beginning of the 19th century. It was in vision of that supersensible action that my Mystery Plays came into being, and for this reason the first Mystery Play, different as it is from Goethe's fairy story of the Green Snake and the Beautiful Lily, nevertheless reveals distinctly similar features. For a thing that would contain real impulses of a spiritual kind cannot be arbitrarily conceived. It must be seen and worked out in harmony with the spiritual world.

Thus we stand here within the Anthroposophical Movement to-day, having entered into the dominion of Michael which has now begun. We stand here in this Movement, called to understand the essence of this reign of Michael, called to work in the spirit of his working through the centuries and the thousands of years. At this moment of great significance he has begun his earthly rulership once more and we are called to work in his direction. Such is the inner esoteric impulse of this stream of Michael, whose working to begin with for this century, is very clearly foreshadowed.

But you must see that if we take Anthroposophy in its present content and trace it backward, we find little preparation for it upon earth. Go back just a little way from what appears as Anthroposophy and try to find its sources in the course of the 19th century, for instance. If you do so open-mindedly, if your vision is not clouded by all manner of philological contrivances, you will not find the sources. You will find isolated traces of a spiritual conception which it was always possible to use like little germinating seeds, though very sparingly, within the great texture of Anthroposophy. But you will find no real preparation for it within the earthly sphere.

All the greater was the preparation in the supersensible. You are well aware how Goethe's working (even after his death, though in my books it may not seem so) contributed to the forming and shaping of Anthroposophy. It is indeed true that the most important things in this respect took place within the supersensible. Nevertheless we can trace the spiritual life of the 19th century backward in a living way till we come to Goethe, Herder, and others, nay even to Lessing. And we find after all that what was working in isolated spirits of the end of the 18th and first half of the 19th century was, to say the least of it, imbued with a strong spiritual atmosphere, even if it appeared in great abstractions as in Hegel, or in abstract pictures as in the case of Schelling.

You may read in my *Riddles of Philosophy* how I described Schelling and Hegel. I think you will recognise that I was seeking to point to something of the soul and spirit in this evolution of world-conceptions which could then enter into the Anthroposophical stream. In the book *Riddles of Philosophy* I tried indeed to take hold of those abstractions of the philosophers with full heart and mind. Perhaps I may specially draw your attention to the chapter on Hegel, and to the things I said of Schelling.

But we must go still deeper to perceive the origin of certain remarkable phenomena that appeared in the spiritual life of the first half of the 19th century. They were lost sight of, they were obliterated in what then came forth as the materialistic spiritual life of the second half of the century. Nevertheless, in however abstract conceptions, there did appear something that contained a hidden spiritual life and being.

Most interesting, and increasingly so the more one enters into him, is the philosopher Schelling. He begins almost like Fichte, with pure, clear-cut ideas, saturated through and through with will. For such was Fichte. Johann Gottlieb Fichte was one of the few figures of world-history—indeed in a certain respect he is perhaps unique—who combined the greatest conceptual abstractions with enthusiasm and energy of will. He is an extraordinarily interesting figure. Short and thick-set, undergrown a little owing to the privations of his youth, one would see him marching along the street with extraordinary firmness of step. He was all will, and will and will again, and his will lived itself out in the description of the most abstract concepts. And yet with these most abstract concepts he could achieve such a thing, for instance, as his *Addresses to the German Nation*, with which he inspired countless people most wonderfully.

Schelling appears in an almost Fichte-like way, not with the same power, but with a similar way of thought. But we very soon see Schelling's spirit expand. In his youth he speaks like Fichte of the " I " and the " Not I " and other such abstractions and inspires the people of Jena with these things. But he soon departs from them. His spirit grows and widens and we see entering into him conceptions, albeit fanciful, which nevertheless tend almost to spiritual imaginations. Thus he goes on for a while. Then he enters deeply into such spirits as Jacob Boehme, and writes something altogether different in style and tone from his former works. He writes *The Foundations of Human Freedom*—which is a kind of resurrection of the ideas of Jacob Boehme.

Then we see almost a kind of Platonism springing up in Schelling's soul. He writes a philosophic dialogue entitled *Bruno* which is truly reminiscent of Plato's Dialogues, and deeply penetrating. Interesting too is another short work *Klara*, wherein the supersensible world plays a great part. Then for a very long time Schelling is silent. His fellow philosophers begin to look on him, if I may put it so, almost as a living dead man. He published only his extraordinarily deep and significant work on the Samothracian Mysteries, once again an expansion of his spirit; but he lives on in simple retirement at Munich, until at length the King of Prussia summons him to lecture on philosophy at the University of Berlin. And of the philosophy he now proclaimed Schelling said that he had gained it in the silence of his retirement through the course of decades.

Now, therefore, Schelling appeared in Berlin, proclaiming that philosophy which was afterwards included in his posthumous works as the *Philosophy of Mythology* and the *Philo-*

sophy of Revelation. He made no great impression on the Berlin public, for the whole tenor of his lectures in Berlin was really this: Man, however much he thinks and ponders, can attain nothing in the sphere of world-conceptions; something must enter his soul, inspiring and imbuing his thought with life as a real, spiritual world.

Suddenly, in place of the old rationalistic philosophy there appears in Schelling a real awakening of the ancient philosophy of the gods of mythology, a reawakening of the old gods in a very modern way, and yet with old spirituality quite evidently working in it. All this is very strange. And in his *Philosophy of Revelation* he evolves ideas of Christianity which do contain, in however abstract a form, important inspirations and suggestions for what must afterwards be said by Anthroposophy, directly out of spiritual vision, on many points of Christianity.

Schelling is most certainly not to be passed over in the easygoing way of the Berlin people. Indeed he cannot be passed over at all, but the Berlin folk passed him over quite easily. When one of his descendants got engaged to the daughter of a Prussian minister (an external, but at any rate a karmically connected event) a Prussian functionary who heard of it remarked: " I never knew before why Schelling ever came to Berlin. Now I know."

Nevertheless one can well come into inner difficulties and conflicts in following Schelling thus through his career. Moreover the last period in his life, dreadfully as it is generally treated in the histories of philosophy, is always dealt with in a chapter by itself, under the title: *Schelling's Theosophy.*

I myself again and again returned to Schelling. For me a certain warmth always proceeded from what lives in him, in spite of the abstract form. Thus at a comparatively early age I entered deeply into the above-mentioned philosophic dialogue *Bruno, or On the Divine and Natural Principle of Things.*

Since the year 1854, Schelling was in the spiritual world again. And he came especially near to one through this dialogue, *Bruno,* if one entered into it, and lived through it,

94

also through his *Klara*, and notably through his essay on the Samothracian Mysteries. One could easily come really near to him in spirit.

And at length, as early as the beginning of the eighteen nineties, it became fully clear to me: However it may have been with the other personalities who worked in the sphere of philosophy during the first half of the 19th century, in Schelling's case it is absolutely clear that a spiritual inspiration did really enter in. Spiritual inspiration worked and entered into his work continually.

Thus one might attain the following picture.—To begin with, down in the physical world, one could see Schelling, as he passed through the manifold vicissitudes of life, through a long period, as I said above, of loneliness and isolation, treated in the most varying way by his fellow men, now with immense enthusiasm, and now again with scorn and derision; Schelling, who really always made a significant impression whenever he appeared again in public—the short, thick-set man, with the immensely impressive head, and eyes which even in extreme old age were sparkling with fire, for from his eyes there spoke the fire of Truth, the fire of Knowledge. And this Schelling whom one can distinctly see—the more so, the more one enters into him—had certain moments when inspiration poured into him from above.

Most clear and visible it became to me when I read Robert Zimmermann's review of Schelling's book on the *Ages of the World*. From Zimmermann, as you know, is derived the word Anthroposophy, though his Anthroposophy is a tangled undergrowth of abstract concepts. I had the very greatest regard for him, and yet, when I read this review, I could not help breaking out into the sigh—" Pedant that you are! "

Then I returned to the book itself, Schelling's *Ages of the World*, which is indeed somewhat abstractly written, but in which one may clearly recognise something like a description of ancient Atlantis—quite a spiritual description, containing spiritual realities, however much distorted by abstractions.

Thus you see in Schelling's case again and again there is something working in from higher worlds, so that we must say: Down there is Schelling, but in the higher worlds something is taking place which influences him from above. In Schelling's case what is a general truth becomes most visible, namely that in spiritual evolution there is a perpetual interplay of the spiritual world above with the earthly world below. And once in the eighteen nineties I was most intensely concerned in finding the spiritual foundations of the age of Michael and of other things.

At that time I myself was entering a phase of life in which I could not but experience intensely the world immediately adjoining our physical world of sense. I could only hint at these things in my autobiography, but I *have* hinted at them there. That adjoining world is separated, if I may so describe it, only by a thin wall from the physical, and in it the most gigantic facts are happening, nor are they at all powerfully separated from our world. It was at the time when I was in Weimar. On the one hand I entered most intensively into the social life of Weimar in all directions; but at the same time I felt the inner necessity to withdraw into myself. These two sides of my life went parallel with one another. And at that time, in the very highest degree, it happened that my experience of the spiritual world was always more intense and strong than my experience of the physical. Already as a young man I had no great difficulty in quickly comprehending any philosophy or world-conception that came into my sphere. But a plant or a stone, if I had to recognise it again, I had to look at, not three or four times, but fifty or sixty times. I could not easily unite my soul with that which in the physical world is named by physical means. And this had reached its highest point during my Weimar period.

It was long, long before the Republican Constituent Assembly took place in Weimar, 'and at that time Weimar was really like a spiritual oasis, quite different from any other place in Germany. In that Weimar, as I said in my autobiography, I did indeed experience intense moments of loneliness. And once again—it was in 1897—wishing to investigate certain matters, I put my hand on Schelling's *Divinities of Samothrace*, and his *Philosophy of Mythology*, simply to receive a stimulation, not in order to study in the books. (Just as one who researches in the spiritual world, if for instance, he wishes to make researches on the periods of the first Christian centres, in order to facilitate matters may lay the writings of St. Augustine or of Clement of Alexandria under his head for a few minutes in succession. You must not laugh about these things. They are simply external methods to assist one, external technicalities that are not directly connected with the real thing itself. They are an external stimulation, like any technical mnemonic.) Thus at that time I took into my hand Schelling's *Divinities of Samothrace* and his *Philosophy of Mythology*. But the real subject of my study at that moment was that which was taking place spiritually in the course of the 19th century, and which afterwards poured down so as to become Anthroposophy.

And at that moment, when I was really able to trace Schelling's life, his biography, his evolution through his life, it was revealed to me—not yet quite clearly, for these things only became clear at a far later date, when I wrote my *Riddles of Philosophy*—it was revealed to me, I could already perceive, although not quite clearly, how much of Schelling's writing was written down by him under inspiration, and that that inspiring figure was Julian the Apostate—Herzeleide—Tycho Brahe. He has not appeared again himself on the physical plane, but he worked with tremendous strength through the soul of Schelling. Then I became aware how greatly Tycho Brahe had progressed in his life as Tycho Brahe. Through Schelling's bodily nature little could penetrate; but once we know how the individuality of Tycho Brahe hovered over him as an inspirer, we read the lightning-flashes of genius in the *Divinities of Samothrace* quite differently. We read the flashes of genius above all in the *Philosophy of Revelation*, and in Schelling's interpretation of the ancient Mysteries, which is, after all, magnificent of its kind. And especially if we enter deeply enough into the curious language he uses in these passages, then presently we hear, no longer the voice of Schelling but the voice of Tycho

Brahe! Then indeed we become aware how, among other spirits, this Tycho Brahe, especially the individuality who was in Julian the Apostate, played a great part, and contributed many things. For by his genius many a thing arose in the spiritual life of modern time which worked in turn as a stimulus, and whence we were to borrow at least the external form and expression for the spirit and teachings of Anthroposophy.

Another of the writings of German philosophers which made a great impression on me was Jakob Froschhammer's book, *Die Phantasie als Welt-Prinzip*, a brilliant book at the end of the 19th century, brilliant because this courageous man, having been driven from the Church, and his writings placed in the Index, was no less courageous in the face of science, for he revealed the kinship of the creative principle of fancy working purely in the soul when man creates artistically, with the force that works within as the force of life and growth. In that time it was indeed an achievement. Froschhammer's book on fancy or imagination as a world-principle, as a world-creative power, is indeed a work of great importance.

Thus I was greatly interested in this man, Jakob Froschhammer. Once more I tried to get at him in a real sense, not only through his writings, and once again I found that the inspiring spirit was the same who had lived in Tycho Brahe and in Julian the Apostate. And so it was in a whole number of personalities in whose working we can see a certain preparation for what then came forth as Anthroposophy.

But in each case we need the spiritual light behind, the light which works within the supersensible. For what came to earth before remained, after all, in a world of abstraction. It is only now and then, in a spirit such as Schelling, or in a man of courage like Jakob Froschhammer, that the abstractions suddenly grow concrete.

And to-day, my dear friends, we may look up to what is working there in spiritual realms, and we may know how Anthroposophy stands in relation to it. And well we know how we are being helped by that which we perceive when we

98

extend our spiritual research into the detailed realities of spiritual life in the course of history. Well may we know it. Here upon earth, striving honestly towards Anthroposophy, there are numbers of souls who have always stood near to the stream of Michael. Added to these, in the supersensible world, are numbers of souls who have remained behind, among them the teachers of Chartres. And between those who are here in the world of sense, and those who are above in the spiritual world, there is a decided tendency to unite their work with one another.

And now if we would find a great helper for those things which we must investigate for the future of the 20th century, if we would find one who can advise us in relation to the supersensible world, if we need impulses that are there within that world, it is the individuality of Julian the Apostate—Tycho Brahe who can help us. He is not on the physical plane to-day; but in reality he is always there, always ready to give information on those matters especially which concern the prophetic future of the 20th century.

Taking all these things together it does indeed emerge that those who receive Anthroposophy in a sincere way at the present time are preparing their souls to shorten as far as possible the life between death and a new birth, and to appear again at the end of the 20th century, united with the teachers of Chartres who have remained behind.

We should receive into our souls this consciousness: That the Anthroposophical Movement is called to work on and on, and to appear again not only in its most important, but in nearly all its souls, at the end of the 20th century. For then the great impulse will be given for a spiritual life on earth, without which earthly civilisation would finally be drawn into that decadence, the character of which is only too apparent.

Out of such foundations, I would fain kindle in your hearts something of the flames that we require, so that already now within the Anthroposophical Movement we may absorb the spiritual life strongly enough to appear again properly prepared. For in that great epoch after shortened life in spiritual worlds we shall work again on earth—in the epoch when for the salvation of the earth the spiritual Powers are reckoning in their most important members, in their most important features, on what Anthroposophists can do.

I think the vision of this perspective of the future may stir the hearts of Anthroposophists to call forth within themselves the feelings which will carry them in a right way, with energy and strength of action and with the beauty of enthusiasm, through the present earthly life; for then this earthly life will be a preparation for the work at the end of the century when Anthroposophy will be called upon to play its part.

Lecture 7

In the lectures to-day and to-morrow I wish to give certain indications which will throw light, not only on the working of karma, but on the wider importance of karmic knowledge for our general knowledge of the history of evolution, especially in the domain of the spiritual life. We cannot understand the real working of karma if we merely consider the successive earthly lives of any one individuality. Certain it is that within this earthly life, being strongly impressed by the earthly career and history of one man or another, or maybe even of ourselves, we are most keen to know: How do the results of former earthly lives reach over into a later one? But the ways of the working of karma would never become clear to us if we stopped short at the earthly lives themselves. For between one earthly life and another man spends the life between death and a new birth, and it is there that karma is elaborated from what has happened in a former earthly life. There it is elaborated in co-operation with other karmically connected human souls who are also in their life between death and a new birth, and with the Spirits of higher and lower Hierarchies. And this elaboration of karma can only be understood if we can look to the world of stars beyond the earth. For we know that the realm of the stars as it appears to physical sight, reveals only its external aspect.

Again and again we must repeat that the physicist would be in the highest degree astonished if he arrived at the places of the stars which he observes through his telescope, whose constitution and substances he analyses with his spectroscope. The physicist, if he were to go to the places where the stars are, would be astonished to see something totally different from what he would expect. For what the star shows to earthly observation is in reality only an outward semblance, comparatively unessential to its own true being. What the star really contains is of a spiritual nature, or, if physical it appears as the remnant, so to say, of something spiritual.

We can best explain this in the following way. Imagine that an inhabitant of some other star were to observe the Earth in the way our astronomers and astro-physicists observe other stars. He would describe a luminous disc shining far out into the cosmos. On it he would find perhaps darker and lighter spots which he would somehow interpret. Probably the interpretation would altogether disagree with what we who inhabit the globe know amongst ourselves. Or perhaps, if Vesuvius were erupting and such a being could observe it, he would theorise that a comet was colliding with the Earth, and so forth. At any rate, what such a being described would have very little to do with the real essence of our Earth.

For what is the essence of our Earth? You must remember that this Earth has proceeded from the Saturn-existence as I described it in my *Occult Science*. In Saturn there was as yet no air, no gas, no liquid, no solid earth-constituent. There were only varied differentiations of warmth. But in those warmth-conditions, everything that afterwards became the mineral, plant and animal, and human kingdoms was contained germinally. We human beings, too, were in the warmth of ancient Saturn.

Then evolution went forward. Out of the warmth, air was precipitated, water was precipitated, and at length the solid element. All these are remnants, precipitated, cast out by humanity in order that it might attain its further evolution. The whole solid mineral world belongs to us. It is but a relic that has remained behind. So, too, the watery and airy elements. Thus the real essence of our Earth is not what we have in the kingdoms of Nature, and not even what we carry in our bones and muscles (for these too are composed of what we have thus cast out and afterwards absorbed again). *Our own souls* are the real essence, and everything else is in reality more or less a semblance, a remnant, a waste product, or the like.

102

The only true description of the Earth would be to describe it as the colony of the souls of man in cosmic space.

Thus are all the stars colonies of spiritual Beings in cosmic space, colonies which we can learn to know as such. And having passed through the gate of death, our own soul lives and moves among these starry colonies. It goes on its further journey, evolving towards a new birth in community with other human souls that are there, and with the Beings of higher or even of lower Hierarchies. And when a man's karma is elaborated and he is ripe to take on an earthly body once again, his soul starts on the returning journey.

To understand karma, therefore, we must return once more to a wisdom of the stars. We must discover spiritually the paths of man between death and a new birth in connection with the Beings of the stars.

Now until the beginning of the age of Michael there have been the greatest difficulties for the men of modern time to approach a real wisdom of the stars. And Anthroposophy, having nevertheless found its way to such a wisdom, must be deeply thankful for the fact that the dominion of Michael really did enter the life of Earth-humanity with the last third of the 19th century. For among many things that we owe to the dominion of Michael there is this too: we have gained once more unhindered access to discover what must be investigated in the worlds of the stars if we would understand karma and the forming of karma in the sphere of humanity.

To introduce you gradually into the extremely difficult questions that arise in the investigation of karma, I will give you an example to-day. It will show you by an illustration how much must be achieved before we can speak of the working of karma as we are doing in these lectures.

It is true enough, is it not, that if we were to speak popularly or in public of the content of these lectures nowadays, these things which are truly an outcome of exact research would be treated as an absurdity. Nevertheless it is a most exact research and you must make yourselves acquainted with all the responsibilities of which one becomes aware in the course of it. You must learn to know all the obstacles and difficulties one meets in such research—the thorny hedges, as it were, which one must pass. For all these things are necessary in order that at length a number of human beings, united karmically in the community of Michael, can learn to know the things of karma. You must know that these are questions of the most earnest spiritual research, far removed from what is imagined by the layman who stands outside this Anthroposophical Movement.

Most of you will remember a character who occurs again and again in my Mystery Plays*—the character of *Strader*. I have already to some extent spoken of these things. The character of Strader is partly drawn from life, in so far as that is possible in a poetic work. I had a kind of pattern for the personality of Strader.† It was a man who lived through the developments of the last third of the 19th century and came to a kind of rationalistic Christianity. After an extremely difficult period of youth (as is suggested in the description of Strader) this man became a Capuchin monk, but he could not bear it in the Church, and at length became a professor.

Having been driven from theology into philosophy, he wrote and spoke with great enthusiasm of Lessing's " free-thinking religion " if one may so describe it. Having come into an inner conflict with official Christianity, he then wanted to found a sort of rationalistic Christianity on a basis of reason and in a quite conscious way. The soul-conflicts of Strader as described in my Mystery Plays did indeed take place in the real life of this man, though of course with certain variations.

Now you know that in the last Mystery Play, Strader dies. I myself, if I now look back and see how I wove the character of Strader into the plot of the four Mystery Plays, must see that though there was no external difficulty in letting him live on just like the other characters, he dies out of an inner necessity at a certain moment. One may well feel his death as a surprise when reading through the plays. But I had the

* The Four Mystery Plays, translated by Adam Bittleston, published by Rudolf Steiner Press, London 1983.
    † Gideon Spicker, 1840–1912.

strong inner feeling that I could no longer continue the character of Strader in the plays.

Why was it so ? You see, in the meantime the original, the model, if I may call him so, had died. Now having based the character of Strader on him, you may well imagine how deeply interested I was in the original, in his further course of evolution. He continued to interest me when he had passed through the gate of death.

Now it is a peculiar thing when we wish to follow the life of a human being clairvoyantly through the time directly after death, through the period that lasts about a third of the physical life on earth. The earthly life, as we know, is in a certain way gone through again backward, at a threefold speed. Now what is the human being really experiencing in these decades that immediately follow his earthly life ?

Imagine a human life here upon earth. We know how it falls into day and night—alternating conditions of waking and sleeping. Already in the periods of sleep man experiences reminiscences of the day-waking life pictorially, but he is not conscious. Ordinarily when we look back upon our life we remember only the day-waking states. Nor do we bear in mind what the chain of memories is really like, for in reality we should say: I remember that day from morning till evening, then there is a break, then again from morning till evening, then again a break and so on. But, as the nights are an empty void in our memory, we draw the line continuously through and thus falsify the chain of memory by placing one day directly after another. After death it is different, for then we must live with intense reality through all the experiences that were present in the *nights* of our life, comprising about a third of the length of our life. We live through it backwards. Now this is the peculiar thing—we have, as you know, a certain sense of reality, a certain feeling of real existence with regard to the things we meet with here in the physical world. If we had not this sense of reality we could consider as a dream all the things we meet with, even in the daytime. Thus we undoubtedly have a sense of the reality of things. We know that they are real; they hit us if we knock against them;

105

they send us light and sound. In short, there are many things that give us our sense of reality here in this earthly life between birth and death.

Now all that we have here on earth as feeling of reality, all that we should describe as the reality—the real existence—of human beings whom we meet here, is in its intensity like the reality of a dream compared to the immensely strong reality which we experience in the decades immediately after death and which the clairvoyant observer can experience with us. For there, everything seems to us more real. The earthly life seems like a dream. It is as though the soul were only then awakening into the real intensity of life.—That is the peculiar thing.

Now as I followed the image of Strader (or of his counterpart) after his passage through the gate of death, the real individuality living after death naturally interested me far more than the reminiscence of his earthly life. For the earthly seems like a dream compared to what emerges after death. Faced with the strong impressions of the dead I could no longer have evolved sufficient interest in the living man to describe his life. In this case I speak out of my own experience. How weak is the reality of earthly life compared with that intensest life which meets us when we follow a man after his death!

When our interest has been kindled on the earth and we try to follow the life of a man in his further course after death, we begin to realise the tremendous difficulties and hindrances. For if we observe rightly and penetratingly, we see, already in that backward course which takes about a third of the time of the past earthly life, how the dead man begins to approach and prepare for the forming of his karma. In a reverse and backward life, he sees all that he underwent during his life on earth. If he offended another man he experiences the event again. If I die at the age of seventy-three, and at the age of sixty I offended someone, I experience it again on the backward journey. But this time I experience, *not* the feelings which I had in giving the offence, but the feelings of the other man. I live right over into him. Thus I with my own experience live in those who were touched in a good or in a bad sense by these my experiences in life. And thus the tendency is prepared and grows in me myself, to create the karmic balance.

Now my interest in the earthly archetype of Strader who now appeared before me as an individuality in higher worlds —my interest in him had been kindled especially by his desire to take hold of Christianity in a very penetrating, in a very brilliant, but rationalistic way. In his case we cannot but admire the thinker, and yet in the books he wrote, in his rationalistic description of Christianity, we see again and again how the thread of rationalism, the thread of abstract concepts breaks at the critical moment, and in the last resort appalling abstractions are the outcome. He cannot really enter a spiritual conception of Christianity. He builds up a religion of abstract philosophical concepts for himself. In short, the whole workings of modern intellectualism find expression in him.

This again appeared in a peculiar way as one followed his path of life after his death. Ordinarily, when there are no special difficulties, we find the human being living gradually into the sphere of the Moon, for that is the first station of the life after death. When we arrive after death in the Moon-region, we find all those whom we might call the "Registrars" of our destiny, who in primeval time were the wise Teachers of humanity. How often we have spoken of them here! As the Moon separated physically from the Earth, and, having been a part of earthly substance, became a heavenly body by itself, so the primeval Teachers of mankind afterwards followed the Moon, and we to-day, when as dead men we pass the region of the Moon, find the great primeval Teachers of mankind. They were not here in physical bodies, but they founded the primeval wisdom of which the traditions of sacred literature are but an echo.

Unhindered, if there are no special hindrances, we find our way after death into that region of the Moon. Now with the human being who was the archetype of Strader, something peculiar occurred. It was as though he was simply unable to approach the Moon-region unhindered and undergo that life

107

of soul which follows directly after death. There were perpetual hindrances, as though the Moon-region simply would not let this individuality approach it.

Then if one followed the real events and causes in pictorial Imagination, the following appeared.—It was as though the Spirits, the primeval Teachers of mankind who had once brought to humanity the original and spiritual wisdom, called out again and again to this human being, the archetype of Strader: " Thou canst not come to us, for owing to thy special qualities as man thou mayst not know anything as yet about the stars. Thou must wait, and first repeat and recapitulate many things that thou didst undergo not only in thy last, but in thy former incarnations. Thou mayst not know anything at all of the stars and their real being, till thou hast thus prepared thyself."—It was a strange scene. One had before one an individuality who simply could not grow out towards the spiritual of the world of stars—or could only do so with the greatest difficulty. And in this case I made the strange discovery that these modern individualities of the rationalistic, intellectualistic mind, find the great hindrance in the shaping of their karma, inasmuch as they cannot approach unhindered the spiritual being of the stars.

On further investigation it appeared that this personality had drawn all the forces of his rationalism from the time that still preceded the dawn of the Age of Michael. He was not yet really touched by the dominion of Michael.

In this case I felt strongly called upon to follow the individual karma farther into the past. It was a real challenge. For I said to myself: something is here, which, working from the results of former lives on earth, has prepared this human being karmically, so that the karma works itself out not only in this earthly life, but extends even into the life after his death. It is indeed a strange phenomenon.

Then the following appeared. The earthly life which I have indicated in bare outline, which is reflected in the character of Strader, this earthly life of the individuality was preceded by a life in spiritual worlds which I can only describe as a sore and grievous trial. It was a trial in the spiritual worlds:

108

" What shall I do with Christianity ? " It was like a slow preparation of the influences which then made him insecure in earthly life in his conception of Christianity. This too shines through in the figure of Strader. He is in no way certain. He rejects the supersensible in a way; he tries only to take hold of it with intellect, and yet after all he wants to *see*. Call to mind the character of Strader, and you will find it so. Thus the real life of the archetype of Strader grew out of his former karma. In effect, in his passage through the life between death and a new birth, before his earthly life at the end of the 19th and beginning of the 20th century, he had passed through the world of the stars in a very dim and darkened consciousness. His consciousness was darkened as he went through that life between death and a new birth. And as a reaction, in his life on earth he conceived concepts the more clear and sharply outlined for the bluntness of the conceptual pictures he had experienced between death and a new birth.

We go backward still—beyond these phenomena which seemed to show the starry worlds as though in a perpetual fog—backward to his former life on earth, and there we find the most remarkable thing of all. We are led to begin with, or at least I was led, to the Battle of the Minstrels in the Wartburg, A.D. 1206. It was the very time of which I told you how the old Platonists from the School of Chartres, for instance, had gone up into the spiritual worlds and the others had not yet descended. It was the time when a kind of heavenly conference took place between the two groups of souls as to the further progress of the activities of Michael. In that time there took place the Battle of the Minstrels in the Wartburg.

It is ever interesting to observe: What is happening here on earth and what is happening yonder? Thus we have an event on earth in the Battle of the Minstrels on the Wartburg, not directly connected with the continued stream of Michael.

Now who was there in the Battle of the Minstrels? The greatest German poets were there together, vieing one with another in their song. The story is well known—how the Minstrels fought for the fame of princes and for their own repute: Walther von der Vogelweide, Wolfram von Eschenbach, Reinmar von Zweter, and how there was one who stood against all the others—*Heinrich von Ofterdingen*.

In this Heinrich von Ofterdingen I found the individuality that underlay the archetype of Strader.

Thus it was Heinrich von Ofterdingen. Now we must concentrate on this: Why did Heinrich von Ofterdingen meet with such difficulties when he had passed through the gate of death? Why did he have to go through the world of stars, as it were, darkened and befogged?

To answer this we must return to the story of the Battle of the Minstrels. Heinrich von Ofterdingen takes up the fight against the others. They have already called the hangman. He is to be hanged if he loses. He manages to withdraw; but, hoping to bring about a renewed contest, he summons the magician Klingsor from the land of Hungary. He did, in effect, bring the magician Klingsor from Hungary to Eisenach. A new Battle of the Wartburg ensues and Klingsor enters the lists for Heinrich von Ofterdingen. Klingsor himself sings against the others, but it is quite evident that he is not battling alone. He causes spiritual beings to battle with him. For instance, in order to do so, he makes a youth become possessed by a spiritual being—and then compels the youth to sing in his place. He calls still stronger spiritual forces into play in the Wartburg.

Over against all that comes from Klingsor's side stands Wolfram von Eschenbach. One of Klingsor's practices is to make one of his spiritual beings put Wolfram to the test, as to whether he is really a learned man. For Klingsor finds himself driven into a corner by Wolfram. In effect, Wolfram von Eschenbach, observing that some spiritual influence is at work, sings of the Holy Communion, the Transubstantiation, the Presence of Christ in the Eucharist, and the spirit is obliged to depart, for he cannot bear it. There are indeed " real realities " underlying these things, if I may use the tautology.

110

Klingsor puts Wolfram to the test, and succeeds indeed, with the help of many spiritual beings, in proving that Wolfram (though indeed he has a star-less Christianity, a Christianity that no longer reckons with the cosmos) is quite unlearned in all cosmic wisdom. This now is the point. Klingsor has proved that the Minstrel of the Holy Grail, even in his time, knows only that Christianity which has eliminated the Cosmic Christianity. Klingsor himself, on the other hand, is only able to appear with the support of spiritual beings, inasmuch as he possesses a wisdom of the stars. But we recognise, from the way he uses his wisdom, that what is called "Black Magic" is indeed mingled in his arts.

In a word, we see Wolfram von Eschenbach, who is a layman in this sphere, encountered by a wisdom of the stars unrighteously applied.

This was in the 13th century, immediately preceding the appearance of those Dominicans of whom I told you. It was at the very time when Christianity, just where it was greatest, had divested itself of all insight into the world of stars. Indeed at that time the wisdom of the stars only existed in quarters that were inwardly estranged from Christianity, as was the case with Klingsor of Hungary.

Now it was Heinrich von Ofterdingen who had summoned Klingsor. Heinrich von Ofterdingen, therefore, had allied himself with an unchristian wisdom of the stars. And thus Heinrich remained united in a certain way, not merely with the personality of Klingsor (who in fact afterwards vanished from Heinrich's life in the supersensible) but with the unchristian cosmology of the Middle Ages. In this way he lived on between death and a new birth, and was reborn as I described it to you. He came into an uncertainty of Christianity.

But the most important thing is this.—He dies again and enters on the returning journey of his life. And in the world of souls, at every step he stands face to face with the necessity, if ever he is to approach the world of stars again, to pass through the grievous battle which Michael had to wage in

111

the last third of the 19th century when he claimed his dominion especially against those demonic powers which were connected with the unchristian cosmology of the Middle Ages.

To complete the picture, I will add that it is clearly possible to see among those who fought hard against the dominion of Michael, and against whom the spirits of Michael had to proceed—it is clearly possible to see among them to this day, the very spirit-beings whom Klingsor conjured up in the Wartburg long ago against Wolfram von Eschenbach.

Thus we see a man whose other results of past karma even led him for a time into the services of the Capuchin Order, unable to come near to real Christianity. He could not come to it because he bore within him the antagonism to Christianity which he had raised in his past life, when he summoned Klingsor to his aid from the land of Hungary, against Wolfram von Eschenbach, the singer of Parsifal. Darkly in the unconscious life of this man the unchristian cosmology still showed itself, but in his ordinary consciousness he evolved a rationalistic Christianity which is not even very interesting. For the interest attaches more to the great conflict of his life, when with a Christian rationalism he tried to found a kind of rationalistic religion.

But it is most significant of all to recognise this connection of abstract rationalism, abstractly clever thinking, with that which lives in the subconscious as darkened, veiled conceptions about the stars and relationships to the stars. Such things, living in the subconscious, rise into consciousness as abstract thoughts. We can study the karma of the cleverest men of the present day—cleverest in the materialist sense— and we find that as a rule in former earthly lives they had something to do with cosmological aberrations into the realms of black magic. This is a very significant connection. An instinctive feeling of it is preserved in the peasants and country folk, who feel a certain aversion from the outset when they find among them someone who is all too clever in a rationalistic sense. They do not like him. In their instinc-ive conception of him there is something which, if we follow it up, belongs to such connections.

Now I want you to consider all these things in relation to our main subject. Such human spirits one could meet with in the last third of the 19th century and in the beginning of the 20th. They are among the most interesting. A reborn Heinrich von Ofterdingen, who had to do with the blackest magician of his time, with Klingsor, proves indeed most interesting in his present-day rationalistic intellect.

We see here how great the difficulties are when one wishes to approach the wisdom of the stars rightly and righteously. Indeed the true approach to the wisdom of the stars, which we need to penetrate the facts of karma, is only possible in the light of a true insight into Michael's dominion. It is only possible at Michael's side.

I have shown you a single example to-day—the example of him who was the archetype of Strader. It will show you once more, how through the whole reality of modern time there has come forth a certain stream of spiritual life which makes it very difficult to approach with an open mind the science of the stars, and the science, too, of karma. But difficult as it is, it can be done. Despite the attacks that are possible from those quarters which I have described to-day, we can nevertheless go forward with assurance, and approach the wisdom of the stars and the real shaping of karma. As to how these things are possible, I will tell you more to-morrow.

Lecture 8

During the past weeks we have been seeking to understand more and more what it means to say that the present age stands in the sign of the dominion of Michael. Thus we were led last time to show how the karma of a human being may work itself out in reality. We showed how difficulties of karma may even go so far that a human being cannot find the way between death and a new birth to live through all that is necessary for the weaving of karma by partaking in the events of the starry world.

So long as our conception is really limited to what happens here in the physical life on earth it is of course difficult for us to receive what we must receive if we are to take the idea of karma in real earnest. But we are living in the age of great decisions and great decisions must take place to begin with in the spiritual field. And in the spiritual field they will be rightly prepared, if out of the deeper anthroposophical spirit, single human beings have the courage to take their study of the spiritual world in real earnest—so much so that they can receive what is brought from the spiritual world and make use of it to understand the phenomena of the outer, physical life.

Hence for a number of months past I have not recoiled from bringing to you detailed facts out of the spiritual life, facts well fitted to enable you to understand the spiritual configuration of the present time.

To-day I will bring forward a few more things as it were to illustrate what I shall then have to say next Sunday, probably in conclusion, showing the whole karma of the spiritual life of the present time in its connection with the tasks and aims of the Anthroposophical Movement.

To begin with, however, I shall bring forward to-day certain facts whose connection with our main subject you will not at once perceive. Nevertheless you will recognise at once how deeply they characterise the spiritual life of the past. Many of these things will seem strange and far-fetched, but life in its totality bears many a paradox, seen from an earthly point of view.

The examples I shall choose to-day are not ordinary ones. For as a rule, a succession of earthly lives is not a continuous succession of historic personalities. It is not generally such that the continuous chain would be visible at all to superficial observation. Nevertheless there are certain successive earthly lives such that if we describe them one after another, we are at the same time giving descriptions of history.

It is seldom the case in such a high degree. But if we do find individualities for whom it is the case, if we can point to the several incarnations as to historic personalities, such an individuality enables us to learn a very great deal about karma. I have already given isolated cases of this kind as you know.

To-day I will tell you about a personality who lived at the end of the first Christian century. Already at that time he was a philosopher. As a philosopher he was most evidently one of the Sceptics, that is to say, he was one of those who really think nothing in the world is certain.

He belonged to that sceptical School which though it already saw the dawn of Christianity, stood altogether on the ground that it is impossible to gain certain knowledge, and above all that it is quite impossible to say with certainty whether a Divine Being could assume a human form or the like.

This individuality—his name in that incarnation is of no great importance, he was a certain " Agrippa "—this individuality in his incarnation in that time, gathered up into himself as it were, the whole of Greek Scepticism. Indeed if we use the word not in a contemptuous sense, but as a technical term, he was one whom we should even call a Cynic. I mean a Cynic not in his conception of life, for in that he was a Sceptic, but a Cynic in his way of taking things. For he was really very fond of making light and joking about

116

most important things that met him in the world. In that life Christianity passed him by, leaving no trace. But a certain mood remained with him as he passed through the gate of death. This mood was not so much a result of his scepticism, for that was his philosophic conviction, a thing that one does not carry very far after one's death. But it lay in the deeper habits of his soul and spirit as an easy-going way of taking important events of life, a certain mischievous delight when things in the world which look important turn out to be not quite so important. This fundamental mood he carried with him into the life after death. Now as I told you yesterday, having passed through the gate of death, man first enters a sphere which leads him by and by into the region of the Moon, where there is the colony of the primeval wise Teachers of mankind. They had once lived on Earth though not in a physical body, nor had they taught in the way we conceive the teaching of later times. They had wandered over the Earth in an etheric body only. And their teaching was such that one man or another who was to receive instruction from them in the Mysteries felt it like an indwelling of these wise Beings of primeval times. He had the feeling: the wise Being has been with me just now. And as an outcome of this indwelling he then felt an inner inspiration. Such was the manner of the teaching given to a human being in those times.

We are referring to the most ancient time of earthly evolution, when the great primeval Teachers wandered upon Earth in their etheric bodies. Then, if we may put it so, they followed the Moon which had already separated as a heavenly body from the Earth. And it is their region which the human being passes, like the first station in his cosmic path of evolution after death. It is they who explain the laws of karma to him, for they have to do with all the wisdom of the past.

Now when the above-mentioned personality, the philosopher " Agrippa," came into that region, it happened that there dawned upon him most intensely, the meaning of a former incarnation. The characteristic of that former incarnation which now made so great an impression on him as he looked back after death, was this, that in it he had still been able to see a very great deal of how the cults of Asia Minor and Africa proceeded out of the ancient Mysteries.

Now in this Christian time in his supersensible life, this individuality went once more, with great intensity, through all that he had once undergone on earth in connection with many a decadent system of the Mysteries in Asia Minor. And so it came about that he now saw supersensibly, how in the ancient Mysteries the Christ had been *expected* (you must remember what I said, that in his life on earth he had not been touched by Christianity).

Now the Mysteries which he had witnessed—I mean the cults that proceeded from the Mysteries—had already grown external. He had in fact received the impressions of cults and religious institutions which were transmitted in the first centuries A.D., in a Christianised metamorphosis of course, to Roman Christianity. Please observe very carefully what I now mean. The point is that in this region after his death, there was prepared in this individuality an understanding for the external features of the cults and clerical institutions which had formerly been Pagan but were arising again in the first Christian centuries and passing over into the clearly defined Roman cult and ceremony with all the ecclesiastical conceptions that were connected with it.

Now this brought about in him a very peculiar spiritual configuration. In the further course of the life between death and a new birth we see him again, elaborating his karma most especially in the region of Mercury, so that he is able to see many things, not in an inward sense but in the sense of being gifted with outward intelligence. He gains a wide sweep of vision for many facts and relationships.

As we follow this individuality further, we find him again on earth. We find him as the Cardinal who carried on the Government of Louis XIV when Louis XIV was still a child, *Cardinal Mazarini*. We may study the Cardinal in all his greatness and splendour and with the external conception of Christianity into which he finds his way so readily, so naturally, under the woman who was Louis XIV's guardian.

118

He absorbs of Christianity all the external institutions, the Christian cult, the Christian pomp and grandeur. For him all these things are surrounded, as it were, with an Eastern glamour as of Asia Minor. Indeed we may say he rules Europe like one who in a former incarnation had strongly absorbed the character of Asia Minor.

But in this life Cardinal Mazarini did indeed have occasion to be more powerfully touched by the facts and circumstances. You need only remember that it was the time of the Thirty Years' War. Remember all the things that took place proceeding from Louis XIV. There was indeed a peculiar quality in this Cardinal Mazarini. He was a great statesman with a wide sweep of vision, yet on the other hand in the midst of a certain noise and confusion. We might say that he was intoxicated by his own deeds so that they seemed deeds of magnificent skill, but not coming out of the depths of the heart.

Now this life took a peculiar course in passing through the time between death and a new birth. We can actually see how in passing again through the region of Mercury, all that this personality had done was dissolved as in a cloud of mist. But there remained with him the ideas he had absorbed about Christianity and all he had undergone by way of scepticism in relation to knowledge. These things were transformed in his life between death and a new birth. " Science can never lead us to the final truths." An intense feeling for knowledge of which there was a suggestion already in his former passage through Mercury, came and passed away again. And there was karmically developed in his life a peculiar mentality. It was a mentality which held fast with great tenacity to penetrating ideas which he had passed through before. But while he held fast to them, he could evolve for his next life on earth very few concepts with which to master and express them. As this personality passes through the life between death and a new birth one has the feeling: Whatever will he try to do in his next incarnation? Is there anything with which he is really united? One has the feeling: he may be more or less intensely united with all kinds of things and

119

yet again with nothing. All the antecedents are there: the preceding life of scepticism, followed by his intense life in a Christianity with all its external details along the paths by which one becomes a Cardinal. All these things are deeply embedded in him. He will become a man rich in knowledge, yet able to come forward with concepts by no means profound. Moreover the map of Europe which he once ruled over is as though blotted out. One does not know how he will find his way to it again. What will he do with it ? He will be altogether at a loss with it.

Yes, my dear friends, we have to enter into such things as these; we have to study what was undergone in passing through the life between death and a new birth in order that we may not err; in order that at length exact and true knowledge may be the outcome.

This personality is re-born in the approaching age of Michael, showing, if I may put it so, a strangely double countenance. He cannot be quite a statesman, nor quite a cleric, but is drawn strongly in both directions. I am referring to *Hertling*, who became Chancellor of the German Reich at a great age. In karmic sequence he had to use up in this way the remnants of his Mazarini nature. All the peculiar qualities with which he came to Christianity, and entered into it, came forth again in his Christian professorship at the present time.

By this example you may see in what strange ways the men of the present time built up their present individualities in past existences.

Anyone who did not research, but merely thought things out, would of course come to absolutely different conclusions. But we only understand karma when we can take these most extreme cases and connections, seeming almost paradoxical in the world of sense. They are there none the less in the spiritual world, even as that other fact is there, which I have often mentioned—I mean that *Ernst Haeckel*, who so violently fought against the Church, is the re-incarnation of Abbot Hildebrand, who became *Pope Gregory*. Here we see how indifferent a matter is the external content of a man's belief or theory in earthly live, for all these things are his thoughts. But if you study Haeckel, especially in connection with what he was as Abbot Hildebrand, as Gregory—(I believe he too is included among these pictures from Chartres)—you will see that there is in fact a real dynamic sequence.

I chose the above example in order that you might see how present individualities carry the past into this present time.

If you will afterwards observe the features of the Monk Hildebrand, who became Pope Gregory VII and whom you know from history, you will see how wonderfully the soul-configuration of Haeckel is contained in this countenance of Hildebrand, of the later Gregory.

I will now take another example, which will probably be of great and deep value to you all. Though I almost shudder to speak of it in any easy way, yet I cannot but choose it, for it leads so infinitely deeply into the whole spiritual texture of the present time.

I will now mention another personality, of whom as I said, I almost shudder to speak in this way. And yet he is infinitely characteristic of all that is carried from the past into the present and of the way in which this happens. I have often referred—and it will be known to you from external history— to the *Council of Nicaea*, which was held in the 4th century, where the decision was made for Western Europe as between Arianism and Athanasianism, and Arianism was condemned.

It was a Council in which the important personalities were imbued with all the high scholarship of the first Christian centuries, and brought it forth. They did indeed dispute with deep and far-reaching ideas. For in that time the human soul still had quite a different mood and constitution. It was as a matter of course for the human soul to live directly within the spiritual world. And they were well able to dispute with real content and meaning as to whether Christ was the Son, of the same essence with the Father, or only of like essence with the Father. The latter was the standpoint of Arianism. To-day we will not go into the dogmatic differences of the question. We will only bear in mind that it was a question of immensely

121

deep and sharp-witted controversies, which were, however, fought out with the peculiar intellectualism of that time. When we to-day are clever and sharp-witted we are so as human beings. Indeed to-day, as I have often said, almost all men are clever. They are really dreadfully clever—that is to say, they can think. Is it not so ? It is not saying much, but it is a fact that they can think: I may indeed be very stupid and still be able to think . . . but the fact is the men of to-day can think. In those times it was not so. It was not that men could simply think, but they felt their thoughts as *inspiration*. He who was sharp-witted felt himself gifted by the grace of God, and his thinking was a kind of clairvoyance. It was still so even in the 4th century A.D., and those who listened to a thinker still had some feeling of the living evolution of his thought. Now there was present at the Council of Nicaea a certain personality who took an active part in these discussions, but at the end of the Council he was in a high degree disappointed and depressed. His main effort had been to bring forward the arguments for both sides. He brought forward weighty reasons both for Arianism and for Athanasianism. And if things had gone as he wished, undoubtedly the result would have been quite different. Not a wretched compromise, but a kind of synthesis of Arianism and Athanasianism would have been the outcome.—One should not construct history in thought, but this may be said by way of explanation.—It would probably have been a very much more intimate way of relating the divine in the inner being of man to the divine in the universe. For, in the way in which Athanasianism afterwards evolved these things, the human soul was very largely separated from its divine origin. Indeed, it was thought heretical to speak of the god in the inner being of man.

If, on the other hand, Arianism alone had won the day, there would of course have been much talk of this god in the inner being of man. But it would not have been spoken of with the necessary depth of reverence, and above all, not with the necessary inward dignity. Arianism alone would indeed have come to regard man at every stage as an incarnation of the god who dwells within him. But the same may be said of any animal, indeed of the whole world, of every plant, of every stone. This conception only has real value if it contains at the same time the active impulse to rise ever higher and higher in spiritual development, for then only do we find the god within. The statement that there is a divine within us at any and every stage of life can have a meaning only if we take hold of this divine in a perpetual *upward striving* of the self, by whom it is not yet attained.

But a synthesis of the two conceptions would undoubtedly have been the outcome if the personality to whom I now refer had been able to gain any decisive influence at the Council of Nicaea. He failed. Deeply dissatisfied, he withdrew into a kind of Egyptian hermitage, lived a most ascetic life, and was deeply imbued at that time in the 5th century with all that was the real spiritual substance of Christianity during that age. Indeed he was probably one of the best informed of Christians in his time, but he was not a wrangler. This is evident from the very way in which he came forward at the Council. He spoke as a man who quietly weighs and judges all aspects of the question, and is yet deeply enthusiastic for his cause, though not for this or that one-sided detail. He spoke as a man who—I cannot say was disgusted, that would not be the true expression—but as a man who felt his failure with extraordinary bitterness, for he was deeply convinced that good would only come for Christianity if the view for which he stood won its way through.

Thus he withdrew into a kind of hermitage. For the rest of his life he became a hermit, following however, in response to the inner impulses of his soul, a quite definite course of the inner life. It was that of investigating *the origin of the inspiration of thought*. His mystic penetration was in the effort to perceive whence thinking receives its inspiration. It became one great longing in him to find the source of thinking in the spiritual world, until at length he was filled through and through with this longing. And with this longing he died, without having reached any real conclusion, any concrete answer during that earthly life. No answer was forthcoming.

123

The time was after all unfavourable.

Then, passing through the gate of death, he underwent a peculiar experience. For several decades after his death he could still look back upon his earthly life, and he saw it forever coloured by that element to which he had come at last. He saw it forever in the atmosphere of that which, looking backwards, came immediately next his death. He saw *the human being thinking*.

Still this was no fulfilment of the question. And this is most important. There was as yet no thought in answer to the question. But though there was no answer, he was able, after his death, to look, in marvellously clear imaginations, into the cosmic intelligence of the universe. The thoughts of the universe he did not see. He would have seen them if his longing had reached fulfilment. He did not see the thoughts of the universe, but he saw *in pictures the Thinking of the universe.*

Thus there lived through the journey between death and a new birth an individuality who was as in a state of equilibrium between mystic imaginative vision and his former sharp-witted thinking—a thinking, however, in perpetual flow, that had not reached its conclusion.

In the elaboration of the karma, his mystic tendency won the day to begin with. He was born again in the Middle Ages as a visionary, a woman, who unfolded truly wonderful insight into the spiritual world. For a time, the tendency of the thinker fell entirely into the background; the quality of spiritual vision was in the foreground. For this woman had wonderful visions, while at the same time she gave herself up mystically to the Christ. Her soul was penetrated, with infinite depth, by a visionary Christianity. They were visions in which the Christ appeared as the leader of peaceful hosts, not quarrelsome or contentious, but like the hosts of peace, who would spread Christianity abroad by their very gentleness—a thing which had never yet been realised on earth. It was there in the visions of this nun. It was a deep, intensive Christianity, but it found no place at all in what afterwards evolved as Christianity in its more modern form.

124

Nevertheless during her life this nun, the seeress, came into no conflict with positive dogmatic Christianity. She herself grew out of it and grew into a deeply personal Christianity, which was afterwards simply non-existent on the earth. And thus, if I might put it so, the whole universe then faced her with the question: how should this Christianity be realised in a physical body in a new incarnation? And at the same time, long after the seeress had passed through the gate of death, there came over her again the echoes of the old intellectualism, the inspired intellectualism. The after-echoes of her visions were now, if I might put it so, idealised through and through, filled with ideas.

Then, seeking for a new human body, this individual became the individuality of Solovioff, *Vladimir Solovioff.*

Read the writings of Solovioff!—I have frequently described the impression they make upon a modern man and have said it again in my introduction to the German edition of his works. You may well try to feel it in his writing. You will feel how much there lies between the lines, how much of a mysticism which we may often feel even sultry and oppressive. It is a Christianity quite individual in its forms of expression. It shows quite clearly how it had to seek for a pliable, in all directions supple body, such as can be obtained only out of the Russian people.

Looking at these examples, I think one may indeed preserve the holy awe and reverence before the truths of karma, which should indeed be held sacred and virginal in the inmost depths of life. For one who has a true feeling for the contemplation of the spiritual world, these deep truths are, verily, not unworthily unveiled. I mean this in the sense of what is so often said about the sacred veils of truth, of which people say that they should never be drawn aside.

Anthroposophy has been reproached again and again, notably in theological circles, for drawing aside the veil of sacred mystery from secret and mysterious truths, and thus making them profane. But the more deeply we enter into the esoteric portions of the anthroposophical conception, the more do we feel that there can truly be no talk of profanation.

On the contrary the world itself will fill us with a holy awe when we behold the lives of man one after another in the marvellous working of former into later lives. We must only not be profane in our inner life or in our way of thinking and then we shall not make such objections.

Read the writings of Solovioff against the background of the previous nun, with her wonderful visions and infinite devotion to the Being of Christ. See that ancient personality going forth with deep and bitter feelings from the Council where he had brought forward such great and important things. Discover in the soul and in the heart of this individual what I may call the twofold background of Christianity, now in its rationalistic, but inspired rationalistic form, and now again in its visionary form of seership. See all this in the background, and of a truth the lifting of the veil will not profane the secret.

A German romanticist once had the courage to think differently from all others about the famous saying of Isis: " I am that which was, that which is, and that which is to come, and my veil has no mortal yet lifted."—To which the German romanticist replied: Then we must become immortal, that we may lift the veil!—While others all took the saying as it stood.

When we discover the truly immortal within us, the divine and spiritual, then may we draw near to many a secret without profaning it, to many a secret to which, with a lesser faith in the divine in our own being, we might indeed not draw near.

And this indicates the spirit which should go abroad ever more and more under the influence of such studies as our last and as this present one. For these spiritual studies are meant to work upon the life and action of those who bear their karma, in the way I have described, into the Anthroposophical Society.

Lecture 9

The lectures I have now been giving under the impression of the presence of so many friends who have come here from different countries, have followed a certain main purpose. Out of karmic sources, I have tried to give a description which should lead, at any rate in a few broad outlines, to a spiritual understanding of the spiritual life of the present time. In a certain respect these lectures will after all form a totality, a single whole, which I will bring to a conclusion in my lecture next Tuesday.

To-day I will give an example to show how difficult it can be to carry into this present time a spiritual science which should really be suited to this time. I will not try to answer the question to-day by reference to external circumstances, but I will answer it by a karmic example. The individuality to whom this example will refer is not exactly typical. It is indeed a very peculiar individuality. Nevertheless this example will serve to show how difficult it is to carry into an earthly life in the present time, what every human being does after all bring with him from his former lives on earth. I mean what he brings with him in the sense that with the possible exception of his very last incarnation, he did after all still stand in original relationship of one kind or another to the spiritual world, or if not in reality, then at least by tradition. And yet in spite of this it is so difficult to carry into the bodily nature of the human being of to-day, into the conditions of present-day education and culture, anything spiritual that was received and absorbed in former time.

To this end I will now unfold before you a succession of earthly lives of an individuality which will reveal to you all manner of hindrances that can indeed arise to prevent the carrying of spiritual contents into the present time. This example will also show you how such difficulties were already prepared in many cases during former earthly lives.

127

To begin with, we will consider a human individuality incarnated in the 6th century B.C. It was the time when the Jews were led into the Babylonian captivity, and a little after that. In studying that period I was struck by an individuality who was incarnated as a woman belonging to the Jewish race. When the Jews were led into captivity, however, that is to say, before they actually arrived in the Babylonian captivity, this woman made her escape. And in the time that followed (she attained a considerable age in that incarnation) she received in Asia Minor all manner of teachings which could be received there at that time. She received among other things what was then living with great intensity, with great impressiveness, even in Asia Minor, elaborating in various directions what we may call the *Zarathustrian world-conception* with its intense dualism. You remember the description in a chapter of my *Occult Science*: the dualism recognising on the one hand Ahura Mazdao, the great Spirit of Light, who sends his impulses into the evolution of mankind, so as to be the source of the good and great and beautiful, who is surrounded by his ministering spirits, the Amschaspands, even as the sun is surrounded in the glory of the manifestation of the countenance of heaven by the twelve signs of the zodiacal circle. These then are the light aspects in the dualism which originated in ancient Persia. On the other hand there was the Ahrimanic opposing power, bearing into the world-evolution of mankind all that is dark, and not only dark but all that is evil, all that hinders and creates disharmony.

This teaching was bound up with the deep and impressive knowledge of the constellation of the stars in the sense of the astrology or astrosophy of ancient times.

All these things, the individuality of whom I am speaking, in her incarnation as a woman in that time, was able to receive because she had as her teacher in a sense, and as her friend, a man who was initiated into many of these doctrines of Asia Minor, and especially also into the Chaldean knowledge of the stars.

Thus we have to begin with a lively interchange of thought

128

between these two, in the period following the abduction of the Jews into captivity. And we have the following remarkable phenomenon. Through the powerful impressions she received, through all the teachings which she absorbed with extraordinary interest and receptivity, powers of seership were awakened in the woman's inner life. She became able to behold the universe in visions which portrayed in a very real sense the cosmic order.

In this case we have to do with a really remarkable individuality. All that had been discovered and experienced between her and the semi-Initiate of Asia Minor who was her friend, all this sprang into life, as it were, within her. And a feeling came over her which we may express in these words: What were all the ideas I received during my instruction as against the mighty tableau of Imaginations that now stand before my soul? How great and mighty is the universe itself, how rich in inner content!—For she realised this through her visionary Imaginations.

This mood gave rise to a certain feeling of estrangement between the two, for the man was more inclined to value the tracing of world-conceptions along the lines of thought, while the woman tended more and more to the pictorial element. Then the two personalities went through the gate of death almost simultaneously, but with a certain feeling of estrangement between them.

Now the results of these two earthly lives became in a strange way fused together. The two individualities went through the most intense experiences in looking backward over their life, in passing backward through their life after their death, and in elaborating their karma between death and a new birth. The result of their life together upon earth was an intense life in community with one another after death.

In the one who had been a woman we find the feeling of preponderance of visionary Imaginations which she had had towards the end of her life no longer present so intensely after her death. Indeed there springs forth in her a kind of longing that in her next earthly life she may comprehend these things

129

more in the form of thought. For in her past life which I have just described she had comprehended them more in the form of speech. From having been livingly experienced in speech they had passed over into the life of visionary Imaginations.

The two individualities, intensely connected as they were with one another in their karma, were reborn in the first Christian centuries at a time when the spiritual substance of Christianity was gradually becoming informed with a certain scholarship and scholarly activity. I have mentioned once before that many of the souls who out of a sincere impulse have since found their way into Anthroposophy, partook in the Christianity of those early Christian centuries. But at that time they could experience Christianity in a far more living form than it afterwards assumed.

Now in this case a peculiar thing appears. There comes before us a man who, as far as karma was concerned, has nothing directly to do with the two individualities of whom I am speaking. But he has to do with them through the history of the time in which they were now living. I refer to Martianus Capella, a dominant personality in the spiritual life of that time. It was he who first wrote the fundamental work on the *Seven Liberal Arts*, which were to play so great a part in all teaching and education throughout the Middle Ages. The Seven Liberal Arts were: Grammar, Rhetoric, Dialectic, Arithmetic, Geometry, Astronomy and Music. In their combined activity and influence they provided what was then felt as knowledge both of Nature and of the Universe.

Martianus Capella's work appears at first sight somewhat dry and matter-of-fact. But we must know that such books, especially in the early Middle Ages, none the less proceeded from spiritual foundations. Indeed this was the case even with those later descriptions which went forth from the School of Chartres, whose apparent character is also dry, enumerating things in categories and the like. In Martianus Capella's descriptions concerning the Seven Liberal Arts and Nature that works behind them, matter-of-fact as they appear

130

to us, we must be able to recognise the outpouring of certain instructive conceptions about higher things. For the Seven Liberal Arts were indeed conceived as real living Being, even as Nature herself was described as a living Being. However apparently dry in their writing, such personalities as Martianus Capella were, none the less, well aware that all these things can be seen in the spirit. Dialectic, Rhetoric, etc. are living Beings, inspirers of human skill, of human spiritual activity. Moreover, as I have explained in these lectures, Nature in her reality, the goddess Natura, was conceived in a similar way to the Proserpina of antiquity.

Now the woman of whom I have just spoken was reincarnated in this time and stood within this stream—within all that arose for mankind under the influence of what was contained in the Seven Liberal Arts, and in the conception of Nature that held sway over them. This time, however, she became a man, who, though in a man's body and a man's intellect, bore within him from the outset the tendency to elaborate whatever was to become his knowledge, not so much in thought, but once more in visionary conceptions.

It may perhaps be said that there were very few at that time, in the beginning of the 6th or at the end of the 5th century A.D.—there were few among those who might be called the pupils of Martianus Capella, in whom the spiritual content of that time lived in a fully vivid, pictorial and living way. But the personality to whom I refer, living now in a male incarnation, could actually speak of his intercourse with the inspiring powers, Dialectic, Rhetoric, and so forth. He was filled with the perception of living, spiritual activities.

And now once more he met the other individuality who had been a man in his former incarnation and who was now a woman, gifted with great intelligence. And once again (we can well imagine how this was karmically conditioned for we witness here the working of karma)—once again there arose an intense spiritual intercourse between them, an interchange, I cannot say of ideas, but of perceptions, a living and powerful assimilation.

But a strange thing arose in that personality who in the

131

pre-Christian centuries had been a woman and was now a man. Because his perceptions and ideas were so vivid, there arose in the man an intense knowledge of how that visionary life which he possessed was connected altogether with the feminine nature. I do not mean to say that the visionary life is in general connected with a woman's personality, but in this case, the whole fundamental character of the visionary life had come over from the former incarnation of the individual as a woman. Thus innumerable secrets were revealed to this man, secrets relating especially to the mutual interaction of Earth and Moon, secrets relating, for instance, to the life of reproduction. The individuality living in this incarnation as a man became remarkably well versed especially in these domains.

Now we see the two individualities passing once more through the gate of death, undergoing the life between death and a new birth, and in their life approaching, in supersensible regions to begin with, the dawn of the Age of Consciousness. For they were still in the supersensible worlds when they experienced the first dawn of the age of the Spiritual Soul. Then the one whom I first described as a woman and in her subsequent incarnation as a man, was reborn as a man once more. It is very interesting that both of them were born once more together, but the other one, who in the former incarnation, i.e., in the second, had been a woman, was now once more a man. Thus both of them were now incarnated simultaneously as men. The one who will interest us especially, who was a woman in ancient time, and a man during the early Christian centuries, who on the first occasion had been of the Jewish race, and on the second had been of extraordinarily mixed blood according to his physical descent, this one was born again in the 16th century as the Italian Utopianist, *Thomas Campanella*, a very remarkable personality.

Let us now look closely at the life of Thomas Campanella in so far as is necessary for an understanding of his karma. He was born with a truly remarkable receptivity for the Christian education which he received. Thus at an early age he began to study the *Summa* of St. Thomas Aquinas. Out of the very moods and feelings which he had acquired through his former visionary life, which became transformed ever more and more into their counterpart—into the impulse to learn to know things in their very forms of thought—he entered with full life into the strong element of thought which is to be found in the *Summa* of St. Thomas Aquinas. Thus he studied with enthusiasm and so became a Dominican in the 16th century.

But into his thinking life which he tries to hold most strictly in the direction in which thought is held in the *Summa* of St. Thomas Aquinas, there enters continually a certain restlessness of that atavistic visionary spiritual life which he had lived before. Thus it is remarkable to see how Campanella actually looked for supports and points of contact in order to bring some inner order and connection into that element which he had once commanded when he had been a visionary in his perceptions of the world. It is remarkable to see how on the one hand Thomas Campanella became a Dominican with full inner enthusiasm. And yet even in the monastery at Cozenza he makes the acquaintance of a very brilliant Jewish Cabbalist. He now combines the study of the Jewish Cabbala with that which emerges as an echo of his former visionary life, and combines it on the other hand with the Thomism which had evolved in the Dominican Order. All these things were living in him with a kind of visionary longing. He wants to do something to bring to appearance outwardly the full inner light of all his spiritual life. You will not find it in the biographies, but so it appears to spiritual vision. There is a perpetual feeling in his soul: Verily the spirit is everywhere behind all things. Surely then in the human life as well there must be a spirit, the same spirit that is in the universal All.

And these things influenced the sphere of his emotions. He lived in Southern Italy. The country was oppressed by the Spaniards. He took part in a conspiracy for the liberation of Southern Italy. For this conspiracy he was taken prisoner by the Spaniards and pined away in the dungeon from the year 1599 till 1626, thus living a life excluded from the world, a life of which one may really say that for twenty-seven years his earthly existence was blotted out.

Now let us place the two facts together.—When he was imprisoned, Thomas Campanella was at the beginning of the thirties of his life, at the very beginning of the thirties. He spent the ensuing time in prison. That is the one thing. But what kind of a spirit was he? What kind of a personality? He set up the idea of a Sun-State, a Solar State. Can you not see shining through from former incarnations into the soul of Thomas Campanella all those astrological conceptions, those visions of the spiritual world? In his work on the Solar State, he conceives and describes a social Utopia, wherein he imagines that by a rational configuration of the social life, all men may become happy. What he thus described as the City of the Sun, or as the Solar State, has about it a certain monastic severity. A good deal of what he has absorbed from the Dominican Order enters into the way he conceives the structure of the State. And extraordinarily much of his former spirituality finds its way through. At the head of this would-be ideal State, there is to be a single leader, a kind of head Metaphysicus who shall discover out of the spirit the guiding lines for the configuration and administration of the State. Other officials shall stand at the side of this Prime Minister, officials who should carry out even to the smallest detail the rules and regulations which a man of that time could only have had in mind if they arose out of his soul through karmic forces as reminiscences of far earlier conceptions of the earth. But in him all these things arose. In effect he wanted to have his Sun-State administered according to astrological principles. The constellations of the stars were to be carefully observed. Marriages were to take place according to the constellations. The acts of conception were to take place in such a way that births might coincide with certain constellations, which were to be calculated. Thus according to the constellations of the heavens the human race with all its destiny should as it were be born on to the earth.

134

Certainly the man of the 19th or 20th century, the neurologist or psychiatrist of the 19th or 20th century, coming across such a work would say: It is fit for the bibliography of lunatic asylums. Indeed, as we shall presently see, the psychiatrist of the 20th century did in a certain respect pronounce a very similar judgment.

Place the two things before your minds. Here is a personality with all the antecedents, the pre-disposing conditions from former earthly lives which I have now described. Out of the power of the sun and stars he wants to bring down and find on earth the guiding lines of the administration of the State. He wants to bring the sun itself into the earthly life, while he himself for more than twenty years pines away in the dark dungeon, and is only able to look out through narrow slits into the sunshine of nature, while in his soul, in very painful feelings and emotions, all manner of things which entered into him in former earthly lives come forth and find expression.—But at length he was set free from prison by Pope Urban. He went to Paris and found favour with Richelieu. He received a pension and lived for the rest of his life in Paris.

And this is the strange thing. The Jewish Rabbi whose acquaintance he had made at Cozenza, through whom his thinking had been coloured in a Cabbalistic way, so that far more became living in him than could otherwise have come to life—this Jewish Cabbalist was the other individuality reborn, the one who had been a man in the first incarnation I described, and in the second a woman.

Thus we see the co-operation of the two individuals, Thomas Campanella and his friend the Jewish Rabbi. And when they have both gone through the gate of death once more, there rises in the individuality who was Campanella in his last life, an extraordinary opposition to what he received in his former lives on earth. His feeling is somewhat as follows. He says to himself: What might not have become of all that if only I had not pined away in the dark dungeon through all those years, looking out through narrow slits into the sunlight of nature ? Yet accordingly there comes over

135

him a kind of antipathy and rejection of what he had before as a spiritual vision, a spiritual conception in the pre-Christian times and in the early Christian centuries. This is the strange thing. While the age of the Spiritual Soul approaches, an individuality goes on evolving in the super-sensible, becoming really hostile to the former spirituality which he possessed. Now it happened thus with very many souls. Even before their earthly life, while they lived through the age of the Spiritual Soul in supersensible worlds, they became hostile to their former spiritual experience. For in effect it is really difficult to carry into a present earthly body what was experienced spiritually in former ages. The present earthly body, the present earthly education, lead the human being into rationalism and intellectuality.

Now this individuality, living on after his life as Campanella, could see no other possibility of creating a true balance than by returning, more or less prematurely, into a new life on earth. Yet the given conditions did not make this easy, for on the one hand even within the supersensible he grew with extraordinary intensity into the element of the Spiritual Soul—I mean the rationalism and intellectualism of the first period in the epoch of the Spiritual Soul. On the other hand, especially when living through again the time of his captivity, his former visionary life and spiritual conception forced its way through ever and again.

Thus the soul of this individuality was laden, as it were, on the one hand with the strong tendency to intellectual enlightenment, repudiating his former spiritual life. Moreover this repudiation gradually assumed a peculiarly personal and individual form. For there arose in him an antipathy to his pre-Christian incarnation as a woman and withal an antipathy to women in general. This antipathy to women found its way into his personality, into his individual life. For so it is with karma. Instead of its being theoretical it becomes a personal concern, personal temperament, personal sympathy or antipathy—in this case, antipathy.

And now the possibility arose for him to live over again in free and open intercourse with the world that earthly life

136

which in his former life on earth as Campanella he had spent in captivity.

Please understand this clearly. On this occasion the other individuality did not accompany him, for the other had no cause to come to earth. In the three preceding earthly lives the Campanella individuality had always had the other one with him to help him to support and guide his life. Now the opportunity arose for him to live once more in an earthly life through all that he had missed by his long years of imprisonment in the life as Campanella. What he had lived through in the darkness of imprisonment gave rise to the possibility of being lived through again in a new life on earth.

What was the consequence, after all the other things had gone before ? Imagine for a moment, when Campanella was thirty years old, or thereabouts, this imprisonment came over him. Imagine the relative maturity of a man in the age of the Renaissance in the thirties of his life. Imagine that what he missed at that time is working again. And at the same time all the other elements, spiritual and rationalistic, are shining in, are raying in from without. Everywhere else and all around is light, only these years of imprisonment are darkness. All these influences are raying in and intermingling: clairvoyance, misogyny, born of the experiences which I described, and in addition, very great cleverness. All these things work into one another in the way they would do as a result of the stage of maturity of a man of the Renaissance in the thirties of his life.

All this is then reborn in the last decade but one of the 19th century or just a little earlier. In the childlike body there is born what is really predestined for a later epoch in man's life. No wonder that the boy—this time it is a male incarnation, for it is indeed only a repetition of the time of his imprisonment; such is the language of karma in this instance— no wonder that the boy is reborn with extraordinary precocity. Of course it is only the forces of growth of a child but working precociously, with the maturity of the thirties of life. —Such is the play of karma, working with all that was missed out of the time of his imprisonment.

137

And a peculiar inclination arises in this belated recapitulation of life, if I may call it so. The old astrological conceptions begin to dawn again, the old conceptions of spiritual life in all Nature which was so wonderful in him in the first Christian centuries. True, these things arise in a childlike way but they live in him so strongly that he has a veritable antipathy to the modern mathematical form of science. In the eighteen nineties he enters the *Gymnasium* or Grammar School. He learns languages and literature magnificently; he does not learn the sciences or mathematics. But the very curious thing is this, so curious as to overwhelm with surprise and joy one who can understand the karmic connections when he sees it—in the twinkling of an eye, beside the other modern languages, French and Italian, he learns Spanish so as to bring into his mentality all that roused his opposition and rebellion against the Spanish dominion in his former life, so as to refresh all this.

See how strangely karma works, how it works into this individuality! It is indeed striking how rapidly the boy learns Spanish, a language remote, outside of his school work, merely because his father happens to have a liking for it. This again is a working of karma. And it signifies a deep influence on the whole mood and attunement of his soul. The fundamental note of imprisonment when anger and indignation against the Spaniards fill his soul emerges in his soul once again now that the Spanish language becomes alive in him and permeates his thoughts and ideas. The very thing that was most bitter for him during his imprisonment now enters the subconscious region where language does in fact hold sway.

Only when he comes to the University does he begin to work at natural science because, in fact, the age demands it. If you would be an educated man in our age you must know something of natural science.

Now I must tell you who it is, for I must relate what happened afterwards. It is none other, then, than the unhappy *Otto Weiniger*.* He makes up for lost time by studying natural

* Otto Weiniger, 1880–1903.

138

science at the University. He studies philosophy at the University of Vienna and takes the degree of Doctor of Philosophy. And in his dissertation he brings forth all that is fermenting in him, fermenting in a way that is only possible when an earthly life is the repetition of an actual gap in the former one. So he writes his dissertation which after attaining his degree he elaborates into a big volume, *Sex and Character*.

In this book *Sex and Character*, all that was there before is boiling and fermenting. Occasionally we see Campanellean utopianism flashing out with ancient primeval conceptions expressed in a most wonderful way.—What is morality? Weiniger answers the question thus. The light that shines forth in Nature is the outer manifestation of morality. He who knows light knows true morality. Hence in the deep-sea fauna and flora which lives without the light we must seek the source of all immorality on earth. And you find wonderful intuitions in his work. For example, he says: Look at the dog, look at its extraordinary physiognomy. What does it show? It shows that the dog has lost something, something is lacking to him; in effect he has lost freedom.

Thus in Weiniger you do indeed find something of spiritual vision combined with the extremest rationalism and hatred of what came to him in a former incarnation. Only this hatred now comes forth not as a hatred of his former knowledge but as a hatred of his incarnation as a woman which finds vent in the misogeny carried to a point of absurdity in the book, *Sex and Character*.

All this will show you how much spirituality can be latent in a soul, how much can have come together with intellectualism in the supersensible world towards the age of the Spiritual Soul and yet it cannot come forth in the present age. It wants to come forth but cannot, even when the present life is no more than the repetition of a period of life that was lost, as it were, in former times.

Strange inclinations arise in Weiniger, extraordinarily significant once more for him who can grasp the karmic threads. His biographer tells us that he acquired the habit towards the end of his life of looking out through very narrow slits which he made for himself from a dark space on to a lighted surface. He took a special delight in doing to. Here you have the time spent in the dungeon, raying in once more into the inmost and most immediate habits of his life.

Think again how Southern Italy was connected with this life, for it was in Southern Italy that all these things had taken place which led him into the present life on earth.

But there is another item which I must mention which is always very important for the student of karma. Needless to say, Weininger too was among the readers of Nietzsche. Imagine the mood and feeling that lived in his soul as he read Nietzsche's *Beyond Good and Evil* and like a bombshell there fell into his soul Nietzsche's statement and further explanation that Truth is a woman. Here indeed what I described to you before comes together coloured by his misogeny.

And now he is twenty-two years old, in the twenty-third year of his life. All these things have worked upon him. Strange habits are evolving in his soul. Is it to be wondered at that a life which is recapitulating a long time of imprisonment is painfully affected by the sunset which reminds him of the oncoming darkness ? Thus Weininger always feels sunsets quite unbearable. And all the time, in his youthful body he has the maturity of the thirties of man's life. I admit that when less talented men are arrogant and vain, it is not beautiful. But here the whole karma can make us understand that he thought much of himself. He had of course various abnormalities, for this life was the repetition of a life of imprisonment when one does not always do the ordinary, normal things, and when one finds karma being fulfilled one may well make the impression of an epileptic on an ordinary psychiatrist. Weininger did make this impression, but his epilepsy was the repetition of the life of imprisonment. His attacks were acts of repulsion and defence. Without meaning in his present life of freedom, they were the karmic repetitions of a life of imprisonment. He was no ordinary epileptic.

Nor need we wonder that in the beginning of the twenties of his life he suddenly and quickly felt impelled all at once and for no reason, to go to Italy. During this journey he writes a wonderful little book, *Über die letzten Dinge*, containing descriptions of elemental Nature which seem almost like an attempt to caricature the descriptions of Atlantis, magnificent, but of course entirely mad from the standpoint of the psychiatrist.

Yet these things must be considered karmically. He suddenly rushes off to Italy, then he returns and spends a short time in the Brunner mountains near Vienna. Having returned from Italy he still writes down a few thoughts that came to him during his journey, magnificent ideas about the harmonies of the moral and the natural world. Then he takes a room in the house where Beethoven died. He lives on for a few days longer in Beethoven's death chamber and now he has finished living through his former imprisonment. He shoots himself. His karma is fulfilled. He shoots himself out of a deep inner impulse, having the idea that if he were to live on he would become a thoroughly bad man. There is no more possibility for him to live, for his karma is fulfilled.

From the point of view which is thus opened out, look at the world of Otto Weiniger, my dear friends. You will see all the hindrances in a soul who is placed so abnormally from the Renaissance age into the present time. You will see all the hindrances that stand in the way and prevent his finding the spiritual, though in the unconscious foundations of the soul he has so much. Now you may draw the conclusion, how many hindrances there are in the Age of Michael to hinder a man from doing full justice to this Age.

For of course it is by no means unthinkable that if the soul of Weiniger had been able to receive a spiritual world-conception he would have been able to continue in his evolution. He need not have put an end to his life by suicide, thus closing the repetition of his life of imprisonment. It is indeed significant to trace in this way how ancient spirituality evolves in souls of men down into modern time and then comes to a standstill. It is just in such interesting phenomena as this that we can see how it is brought to a standstill.

I think indeed that this will illumine certain karmic connections in the spiritual and intellectual life of the present time. It will enable us to look more deeply into the karmic relationships, now that we have placed before us these four successive incarnations of an extraordinarily interesting individuality, incarnations extending from the 6th century before the Mystery of Golgotha until to-day. That indeed is the span of time including all that we must study if we would understand the life of our own time.

To-day we have taken a case which teaches us how many things a soul can undergo during this age. I would far rather describe these things by the concrete experiences of the soul than by abstract explanations.

I will close the present cycle of lectures next Tuesday evening which will indeed be the last of these lectures to Members.

Lecture 10

From our last lecture you will at any rate have seen that the man of to-day, constituted as he is in his bodily nature and by education, cannot easily bring into his present incarnation such spiritual contents as are seeking to enter in from former incarnations. He cannot even do so when this present incarnation is so strange and unusual a one as that of which I spoke last Sunday. For, in effect, we are living in the age of evolution of the conscious, spiritual soul. This is an evolution of the soul which evolves most especially the intellect, i.e., that faculty of the soul which governs the whole of life to-day, no matter how often people may be crying out for heart and sentiment and feeling. It is the faculty of the soul which is most able to emancipate itself from the elementarily human qualities, from that which man bears within him as his deeper being of soul.

A certain consciousness of this emancipation of the intellectual life does indeed find its way through when people speak of the cold intellect in which men express their egoism, their lack of sympathy and compassion with the rest of mankind, nay even with those who are nearest to them in their life. Speaking of the coldness of the intellect one has in mind the following of all those paths which lead, not to the ideals of the soul, but to the planning of one's life on utilitarian principles and the like.

In all these things people give expression to a feeling of how the element of intellect and rationalism emancipates itself within the human being from what is truly human. And indeed if one can fully see the extent to which the souls of to-day are intellectualised, one will understand also in every single case how karma must carry into the souls of to-day the high spirituality which these souls have passed through in former epochs. For I ask you to consider the following.—Let us take quite a general case. I showed you a special

143

example last time, but let us now take the general case of a soul that lived in the centuries before the Mystery of Golgotha or even after the Mystery of Golgotha in such a way as to take the spiritual world absolutely a matter of course. Let us think of a human being who in such a life could speak of the spiritual world out of his own experience as of a world that is no less real and present than the many-coloured warm and cold world of the senses.

All these things are there within the soul. And in the interval between death and a new birth, or in repeated intervals of this kind, all these things have entered into relationship with the spiritual worlds of higher Hierarchies. Many and manifold things have been worked out in such a soul.

But now, let us say through other karmic circumstances, such a soul has to incarnate in a body which is altogether attuned to intellectualism, a body which can receive from the civilisation of to-day only the current conceptions which relate, after all, only to external things. In such a case this alone will be possible, for the present incarnation: the spirituality that comes over from former times will withdraw into the subconscious. And such a personality will reveal in the intellect which he evolves perhaps a certain idealism, a tendency to all manner of good and beautiful and true ideals. But he will not come to the point of lifting up from the subconscious into the ordinary consciousness the things that are there latent in his soul. There are many such souls to-day. And for him who is truly able to observe with a trained eye for spiritual things, many a countenance to-day will contradict what openly comes forth in him who wears it. For the countenance says: in the foundations of the soul there is much spirituality, but as soon as the human being speaks, he speaks not of spirituality at all. In no age was it the case in such a high degree as it is to-day, that the countenances of men contradict what they themselves say and declare.

We must understand that strength and energy, perseverance and a holy enthusiasm are necessary in order to transform into spirituality the intellectualism which after all belongs to the present age. These things are necessary that

144

the thoughts and ideas of men to-day may rise into the spiritual world and that man may find the path of ideas upward to the Spirit no less than downward into Nature. And if we would understand this, then we must fully realise that intellectualism to begin with offers the greatest imaginable hindrance to the revelation of any spiritual content that is present within the soul. Only when we are really aware of this, only then shall we, as Anthroposophists, find the true inner enthusiasm. Then shall we receive on the one hand the ideas of Anthroposophy which must indeed reckon with the intellectualism of the age, which must remain, so to speak, the garment of contemporary intellectualism. Then shall we also become permeated with the consciousness that with the ideas of Anthroposophy, relating as they do, not to the mere outer world of sense, we are destined really to take hold of that to which they do relate, namely, the spiritual. To enter deeply and perseveringly into the ideas of Anthroposophy—it is this in the last resort which will most surely guide the man of to-day upward into spirituality, if only he is willing.

But what I have said in this last sentence, my dear friends, can truly only be said since about the last two or three decades. Previously one could not have said it. For although the dominion of Michael began already with the end of the seventies, nevertheless it was formerly the case that the ideas which the age provided were so strongly and exclusively directed to the world of sense that even for the idealist to rise from intellectualism to spirituality was possible only in rare, exceptional cases in the seventies, eighties and nineties of the last century.

To-day I will give you an example to reveal the outcome of this fact. I will show you by an example how strong and inevitable a force is working in this age to drive back and dam up the spiritual contents which are surging forth from former times in human souls. Nay, at the end of last century such spiritual contents had to withdraw and give way to intellectualism if they were to be able to reveal themselves in any way at all.

145

Please understand me rightly. Let us assume that some personality living in the second half of the 19th century bore within him a strong spirituality from former incarnations. Such a personality lives and finds his way into the culture and education of this present time (or of that time) which is intellectualistic, thoroughly intellectualistic. In the personality whom I now mean, the after-working of former spirituality is still so strong that it is really determined to come forth, but the intellectualism will not suffer it. The man is educated intellectually. In the social intercourse which he enters into, in his calling or profession, everywhere he experiences intellectualism. Into this intellectualism what he bears within his soul cannot enter. Such a human being would be one of whom we might say that Anthroposophy would truly have been his calling. But he cannot become an Anthroposophist, though the very thing which he bears within him from a former incarnation, if it could enter into the intellect, would have become Anthroposophy. It cannot become Anthroposophy; it stops short; it recoils as it were from intellectualism. What else can such a personality do ? At most he will treat intellectualism again and again as a thing into which he does not really want to enter, so that in one incarnation or another what he bears within his soul may be able to come forth. Of course it will not come forth completely, for it is not according to the age. It will very likely be a kind of stammering; but it will be visible in such a man how he recoils and shrinks again and again from going too far, from being touched too closely by the intellectualism of the age.

I want to give you an example of this very thing to-day. To begin with I will remind you of a personality of ancient time whom we have mentioned here again and again in all manner of connections, I mean, *Plato*. In Plato the philosopher of the 5th and 4th centuries B.C. there lives a soul who forestalls many of the things that mankind ponders on for centuries to come. You will remember when I drew your attention to the great spiritual contents of the School of Chartres, how I referred to the Platonic spirit which had been living for a long time in the development of Christianity. And in a certain sense it was in the great teachers of Chartres that this Platonic spirit found its true development according to the possibilities of that time.

We must realise that the spirit of Plato is devoted in the first place to the world of Ideas. We must not, however, conceive that the " Ideas " in Plato's works are the abstract monster which ideas are for us to-day, if we are given up to the ordinary consciousness. For Plato, the " Ideas " were to some extent almost what the Persian Gods had been, the Amshaspands who as active genii assisted Ahura Mazdao. Active genii attainable only in imaginative vision—such in reality were the Ideas in Plato. They had a quality of being, only he no longer described them with the vividness with which such things had been described in former times. He described them as it were like the shades of beings. Indeed this is how abstract thoughts henceforth evolved: the Ideas were taken by human beings in an ever more and more shadow-like way. But Plato, as he lived on, nevertheless grew deeper in a certain way, so that one might say: well-nigh all the wisdom of that time poured itself out into his world of Ideas. We need only take his later Dialogues, and we shall find matters astronomical, astrological, cosmological, psychological, the last named expressed in a most wonderful way, and matters concerning the history of nations. All these things were found in Plato in a kind of spirituality which, if I may so describe it, refines and shadows down the spiritual to the form of the Idea.

But in Plato everything is alive, and in Plato above all this perception is alive: that the Ideas are the foundations of all things present in the world of sense. Wherever we turn our gaze in the world of sense, whatever we behold, it is the outward expression and manifestation of Ideas.

Withal there enters into Plato's world of conception yet another element which has indeed become well known to all the world in a catchword much misunderstood and much misused—I mean the catchword of Platonic love. The love that is spiritual through and through, that has laid aside as

147

much as possible of that egoism which is so often mingled with love—this spiritualised devotion to the world, to life, to man, to God, to the Idea, is a thing that permeates the Platonic conception of life through and through. It is a thing which afterwards recedes in certain ages only to light up again repeatedly. For Platonism is absorbed by human beings ever and again. Again and again at one place or another it becomes the staff by which men draw themselves upward. And Platonism, as we know, entered most significantly into all that was taught in the School of Chartres.

Plato has often been regarded as a kind of precursor of Christianity. But to imagine Plato as a precursor of Christianity is to misunderstand the latter, for Christianity is not a doctrine, it is a stream of life which takes its start from the Mystery of Golgotha. It is only since the Mystery of Golgotha that we can speak of a real Christianity. We can however say that there were Christians before the Mystery of Golgotha in this sense, that they revered as the Sun Being and recognised in the Sun Being the sublime Figure who was subsequently recognised as the Christ within the earthly life of mankind. If, however, we speak of precursors of Christianity in this sense we must apply the term to many pupils of the ancient Mysteries, among whom we may indeed include Plato. Only we must then understand the thing aright.

Now I already spoke at this place some time ago of a young artist who grew up while Plato was still living, not exactly in Plato's School of the Philosophers but under Plato's influence. Indeed I mentioned this matter already many years ago. Having passed through other incarnations in the meantime this individuality was reborn, not out of the Platonic philosophy but out of the Platonic spirit. He was reborn as *Goethe*, having karmically transformed in the Jupiter region what came to him from former incarnations, and notably from the one in which he partook of the Platonic stream, so that it became that kind of wisdom which does indeed permeate all the contents of Goethe's work. Thus we can indeed turn our gaze to a noble and pure relationship

148

between Plato and this—I will not say " disciple "—but follower of Plato. For as I said, he was not a philosopher but an artist in that Grecian incarnation. Nevertheless Plato's eye did fall upon him and perceived the infinite promise that lay within this youth.

Now it was truly hard for Plato to carry through the following epochs, through the supersensible world, what he had borne within his soul in his Plato incarnation. It was very hard for him. For although Platonism lit up here and there, when Plato himself looked down upon the Platonism that evolved here on the earth, it was for him only too frequently a dreadful disturbance in his supersensible life of soul and spirit.

I do not mean that that which lived on as Platonism was therefore to be condemned or harshly criticised. Needless to say the soul of Plato carried over livingly into the following epochs piece by piece and ever more and more, what lay within him. But Plato above all, Plato who was still united with the Mysteries of antiquity, of whom I said that his Doctrine of Ideas contained a certain ancient Persian impulse—Plato found the greatest difficulty in entering a new incarnation. When he had absolved the time between death and a new birth—and in his case it was a fairly long time—he found real difficulty in entering the Christian epoch into which, after all, he had to enter. Thus although in the sense I just explained we may describe Plato as a forerunner of Christianity, nevertheless the whole orientation of his soul was such as to make it extraordinarily difficult for him, when ready to descend to earth again, to find a bodily organism into which he might carry his former impulses in a way that they might now come forth again with a Christian colouring.

Moreover Plato was a Greek. He was a Greek through and through, with all those oriental impulses which the Greeks still had, which the Romans had not at all. Plato was in a certain sense a soul who carried philosophy upwards into the higher poetic realm. The Dialogues of Plato are works of art. Everywhere is the living soul, everywhere the Platonic

149

love which we need only understand in the true sense and which also bears witness to its oriental origin.

Plato was a Greek, but the civilisation within which alone he could incarnate, now that he was ripe for incarnation, now that he had grown old for the supersensible world—this civilisation was Roman and Christian.

Nevertheless, if I may put it so, he must take the plunge. And to repress the inner factors of opposition, he must gather together all his forces. For it lay in Plato's being to reject the prosaic, matter-of-fact and legalistic Roman element, nay indeed to reject all that was Roman.

And there was also a certain difficulty for his nature to receive Christianity, for he himself represented in a certain sense the highest point of the pre-Christian conception of the world. Moreover even the external facts revealed that the real Plato-being could not easily dive down into the Christian element. For what was it that dived down into Christianity here in the world of sense ? It was Neo-Platonism, but this was something altogether different from true Platonism. We remember how there evolved a kind of Platonising Gnosis and the like but there was no real possibility of taking over into Christianity the immediate essence of Plato. Thus it was difficult for Plato himself, out of all the activity which he bore within him as the Plato-being and the results of which he must now bring with him into the world—it was difficult for him to dive down in any way. He had as it were to reduce all this activity.

And so it was that he reincarnated in the 10th century in the Middle Ages as the nun *Hroswitha*—Hroswitha, that forgotten but great personality of the 10th century, who did indeed receive Christianity in a truly Platonic sense and who carried into the Mid-European nature very, very much of Plato.

She belonged to the Convent of Gandersheim in Brunswick and carried infinitely much of Platonism into the Mid-European nature. This in truth it was only possible at that time for a woman to do. Had not Plato's being appeared with a feminine character and colouring it could not have

150

received Christianity into itself in that age. But the Roman element too was strong in all the culture of that time which had to be received. Perforce, if I may put it so, it had to be received. And so we see the nun Hroswitha evolving into the remarkable personality she was, writing Latin dramas in the style of the Roman poet Terence, dramas which are of extraordinary significance.

You see, it is appallingly easy to misrepresent Plato wherever he approaches one. I often described how Friedrich Hebbel made notes of a play—it never got beyond the plan—Friedrich Hebbel made notes of a play in which he would give a humorous treatment of the following theme.—Plato reincarnated sits on the benches of a grammar school.—A mere poetic fancy, needless to say, but this was Hebbel's idea.—Plato is reincarnated as a schoolboy while the school-master puts him through the Platonic Dialogues and Plato himself, reincarnated, receives the very worst criticism with respect to the interpretation of the Platonic Dialogues. These things Hebbel noted down as the subject for a play which he never elaborated. Nevertheless it shows, it is like a divination of how easy it is to misunderstand Plato. Now this is a feature which interested me most especially in tracing the stream of Plato. For this very misunderstanding is extra-ordinarily instructive in finding the right paths of the further life and progress of the Platonic individuality.

It is indeed highly interesting. There was a German philosopher (I do not remember his name, it was some Schmidt, or Müller), who with all his scholarship " proved " up to the hilt that the nun Hroswitha wrote not a single play, that nothing was due to her, that it was all a forgery by some Counsellor of the Emperor Maximilian. All of which proof is of course nonsense, but there you have it. Plato cannot escape misunderstanding.

And so we see arising in the individuality of the nun Hroswitha of the 10th century, a truly intensive Christian and Platonic spiritual substantiality united with the Mid-European-Germanic spirit. And in this woman there was living so to speak the whole culture of that time. She was indeed an astonishing personality. And she among others partook in those supersensible developments of which I told you. I mean the passage of the teachers of Chartres into the spiritual world, the descent of those who were then the Aristotelians, and the discipleship of Michael. But she took part in all these things in a most peculiar way. One may say: here was the masculine spirit of Plato and the feminine spirit of the nun Hroswitha wrestling with one another, inasmuch as they both of them had their results for the spiritual individuality. If the one incarnation had been of no significance, as is generally the case, such an inward wrestling could not afterwards have taken place. But in this individuality it did take place and indeed it went on for the whole succeeding time.

And at length we see the individuality ripe to return to earth once more in the 19th century. He became an individuality of the very kind I described above as a hypothetical case. For the whole spirituality of Plato is held back, recoils and shrinks back in the face of the intellectuality of the 19th century which it will not come near.

And to make this process the easier the feminine capacity of the nun Hroswitha has been instilled into the same soul. Thus as the soul appears on the scene, all that it had received from its incarnation as a woman, great and radiant as she was, makes it the more easy to repel the modern intellectualism wherever it is not liked.

Thus the individuality stands upon earth anew in the 19th century. He grows up into the intellectuality of the 19th century but lets it come near him only to a certain extent, externally, while inwardly he is perpetually shrinking back from it. Platonism comes forward in his consciousness not in an intellectualistic way, for again and again, wherever he can, he speaks of how Ideas are living in all things.

The life in Ideas became an absolute matter of course to this personality. Yet his body was such that one continually had the following impression: the head simply cannot give expression to all the Platonism that is seeking to come forth in him. But on the other hand there could spring forth in him in a beautiful way, nay in a glorious way, that which is hidden behind the word " Platonic Love."

Nay more, in his youth this personality had something like a dream-intuition of how Mid-Europe cannot and may not after all be truly Roman. For indeed he himself had lived as the nun Hroswitha. Thus in his youth he represented Mid-Europe as a modern Greece. Here we see his Platonism striking through. And he represented the rougher region that had stood over against ancient Greece, namely Macedonia, as the present East of Europe. There were strange dreams living in this personality, dreams from which one could see, and this was very interesting, how he wanted to conceive the modern world in which he himself was living, like Greece and Macedonia. Again and again, especially in his youth, there arose the impulse to conceive the modern world—Europe on a large scale—as Greece and Macedonia magnified.

The personality of whom I am speaking is none other than *Karl Julius Schröer.* With the help of all that I have now brought together you need only take Karl Julius Schröer's writings. From the very beginning he speaks in a thoroughly Platonic way. But this is so strange: with a kind of feminine coyness, I might say, he takes good care not to enter into intellectualism wherever he has no use for it.

When he spoke of Novalis, Schröer was often fond of saying: Novalis—he is a spirit whom one cannot understand with this modern intellectualism which knows only that twice two is four.

Karl Julius Schröer wrote a history of German poetry in the 19th century. In this history, wherever one can approach a thing with Platonic feeling, it is very good, but wherever one requires intellectualism it is suddenly as though the lines were to sink away into nothingness. He is not a bit like a professor. He writes many pages about some who are passed over in silence by the ordinary histories of literature, while about the famous ones he sometimes writes only a few lines.*

* There is a gap in the stenograph here. According to some who attended the lecture, Rudolf Steiner spoke of Christian

153

When this history of literature was first published, how the literary pundits did wring their hands! One of the most eminent among them at that time was Emil Kuh, who declared: this history of literature is not written by a head at all; it simply flowed out of a wrist.

Karl Julius Schröer also published an edition of *Faust*. A professor—in Graz—for the rest a very good fellow—wrote such a dreadful review of it that I believe no less than ten duels were fought out among the students at Graz pro and contra Schröer.

There was indeed much grievous misunderstanding, failure of recognition. This poor estimate of Schröer went so far that on one occasion at a social gathering in Weimar where I was present, the following thing happened. In that circle Erik Schmidt was a highly respected personality and dominated everything when he was present. Conversation turned on the question, which of the princesses and princes at the Weimar Court were wise and which were stupid. This was being seriously discussed and Erik Schmidt declared: the Princess Reuss (she was one of the daughters of the Grand Duchess Reuss)—the Princess Reuss is not a clever woman for she considers Schröer a great man.—This was his reason!

But you must go through all his works, down to that most beautiful little book *Goethe und die Liebe*, for there you will really find what one can say without intellectualism about Platonic Love in immediate and real life. Something extraordinary is given to us in the style and tone of this little book *Goethe und die Liebe*. It came to me beautifully on one occasion when I was discussing the book with Schröer's sister. She called the style "völlig süss vor Reife", fully sweet unto ripeness—a pretty expression. And such indeed it is. It is all —I cannot say in this sense so concentrated—but it is all so fine, so delicate in its form. Refinement indeed was a peculiar quality of Schröer's.

And yet this Platonic spirituality, repelling intellectualism,

Oeser, the father of Karl Julius Schröer, as being the reincarnation of Socrates.

154

this Platonic spirituality that did not want to enter into this body made at the same time a quite peculiar and strong impression, for in seeing Schröer one had the distinct perception: this soul is not quite fully there within the body. And then when he grew older one could see how the soul, not being really willing to enter into the body of that time, withdrew little by little out of that body. To begin with the fingers grew swollen and thick. Then the soul withdrew ever more and more, and as we know, Schröer ended in the feeble-mindedness of old age. Certain features of Schröer, not the whole individuality, but certain features, were taken over into my character Capesius, Professor Capesius, in the Mystery Plays.

Here indeed we have a remarkable example of the fact that the spiritual currents of antiquity can only be carried over into the present time under certain conditions. And one may well say that in Schröer the recoiling from intellectuality showed itself characteristically. Had he attained intellectuality, had he been able to unite it with the spirituality of Plato, Anthroposophy itself would have been there.

And so we see in his karma how his paternal love for his follower Goethe, if so I may describe it, becomes transformed. It had arisen in the way I told you, for in that ancient time Plato had indeed loved him in a paternal way. We see this love karmically transmuted; Schröer becomes a warm admirer of Goethe. Thus it emerges once again.

There was something extraordinarily personal in Schröer's reverence for Goethe. In his old age he wanted to write a biography of Goethe. Before I left Vienna at the end of the eighties he told me about it and afterwards he wrote me about it. But of this biography of Goethe which he would have liked to write he never wrote in any different vein than this.—He said: Goethe is continually visiting my soul. It always had this personal character which was indeed karmically predestined as I have now indicated.

The biography of Goethe was never written, for Schröer fell into the feeble-mindedness of old age. But we can indeed find a luminous interpretation of the whole character of his writings if we know the antecedent which I have now explained.

Thus in the well-nigh forgotten character of Schröer, we see how Goetheanism came to a standstill before the threshold of intellectualism transformed into spirituality. And if I may put it so, one could really do no other, having once been stimulated by Schröer, than carry Goetheanism forward into Anthroposophy. There was no other course to take. And again and again this deeply moving picture (for so it was for me) stood before the eye of my soul: Schröer carrying the ancient spirituality of Goethe, pressing forward in it up to the point of intellectuality. And I understood how Goethe must be grasped again with modern intellectualism, lifted up into the spiritual domain. For only so shall we fully understand him. Nor did this picture by any means make things easy for me. For owing to the fact that that which Schröer was could not directly and fully be received, again and again there was mingled in the striving of my soul, a certain element of opposition against Schröer.

Thus, for example, when at the Technical University in Vienna Schröer conducted practice classes in lecturing and essay writing, I once gave a pretty distorted interpretation of Mephisto merely to refute my instructor Schröer with whom at that time I was not yet on such intimate and friendly terms. There was indeed a certain opposition stirring within me.

But as I said, what else could one do than loose the congestion that had taken place and carry Goetheanism really onward into Anthroposophy!

Thus you see how world-history really takes its course. For it takes its course in such a way that we may recognise: whatever we possess in the present day emerges with great hindrances and difficulties. Yet on the other hand it is well prepared.

Read the wonderful hymn-like descriptions of womanhood in Karl Julius Schröer's writings. Read the beautiful essay which he wrote as an appendix to his *History of Literature,* his *History of German Poetry in the 19th Century.* Read his essay on Goethe and his relation to women. If you take

156

all these things together you will say to yourselves: truly here is living something of a feeling of the worth and character of womanhood which is an echo of what the nun Hroswitha had lived as her own being. These two preceding incarnations harmonise and vibrate together wonderfully in Schröer's life, so much so that the breaking of the thread became indeed a deeply moving tragedy. And yet in Schröer of all people there enters into the end of the 19th century a world of spiritual facts, immensely illuminating towards an answer to this question: *How shall we bring spirituality into the life of the present time?*

Herewith I wished to round off this cycle of lectures.

Preface to "The Last Address'

Autumn in Dornach can be incomparably beautiful. Even spring-time when all the cherry trees around the Goetheanum are in blossom cannot match it. In autumn the gardens abound with flowers in every possible colour and shape, the clear air blows down from the Alps—they cannot be seen but their presence is felt in the background; the autumn sun fills the valleys with a steady, warm glow; in the stillness of the night the stars glitter overhead and seem to send messages to those who can hear them and the whole atmosphere is filled with a sense of ripeness, fulfilment and fruitfulness.

It was in such a setting that Rudolf Steiner achieved the fantastic culmination of his twenty-five years of anthroposophical work. As will be generally known, he gave the results of his studies and investigations mainly in lectures. The shorthand records of nearly six thousand of them have been preserved. The living contact from spirit to spirit through the spoken word proved to be the best means of getting over those astonishing discoveries in the spirit-world which he had made in long years of earnest and innermost research. Of course, the books which he wrote and prepared for publication with their concentrated, limpid, crystal-clear style are indispensable for the study of Anthroposophy. But in his lectures the very pulse of his own spiritual life could be felt and in some measure can still be recaptured in the published notes and transcripts.

In the last autumn of his life, during the month of September 1924, Rudolf Steiner surpassed in sheer concentrated quantity anything he had ever done before. Of the quality of these last gifts it is difficult to speak; ordinary words do not measure up to it.

He gave four lectures every day, sometimes even five, during those September weeks. In the evening he spoke to members of the Anthroposophical Society on the delicate subject of Reincarnation and Karma. A supreme master of the subject, he understood how to lift in some measure the veil from the age-old spiritual-historic background of the Anthroposophical Movement. Or he would assemble the members of the Esoteric School for a special class. In the mornings and afternoons three courses continued from day to day. A series of eighteen lectures on the Book of Revelation was given to the priests of the Christian Community; a series of lectures on Pastoral Medicine to anthroposophical doctors and the priests together; a series of nineteen lectures on Dramatic Art to the students of speech and drama at the Goetheanum. In this last course he sometimes took whole scenes from Plays and acted them himself, impersonating one character after another. On two days of the week he also continued his regular lectures for the workmen at the Goetheanum.

As one who was privileged to take part in all these courses and lectures except those for the workmen, I would testify to the truly extraordinary combination of sober matter-of-factness and spiritual elation which prevailed in these meetings. The flood-gates of Revelation were opened as they had not been for uncounted times, and yet it was all taken as part of normal human life.

In the evening of Friday 27th September we made our way as usual up the hill to the *Schreinerei*, the large carpenter's workshop where most of the wooden structure for the first Goetheanum had been prepared, and where a temporary lecture-hall had been improvised after the first Goetheanum had been destroyed by fire and while the second Goetheanum was being built. For the first time in Rudolf Steiner's life a brief notice was put up to say that he was unable to give his lecture that night because he was not well enough to do so.

Reports and rumours concerning his health had been current for some time. Spiritual development and transformation of the kind Rudolf Steiner achieved draws on the natural vitality of the body in a manner in which a lighted candle consumes its substance as a sacrificial flame. As a result, the digestive system grows extremely sensitive. It was said that with Rudolf Steiner this had reached such a degree that at times ordinary food would affect him like poison. It was also said that with the burning of the first Goetheanum part of his very own life had gone away with the flames. Indeed one could not fail to notice with growing anxiety that at times he looked exhausted.

On the previous day, 26th September, I had been allowed to call on him briefly on a private matter, and was deeply distressed to see him as I had never seen him before. I hardly dared to speak. I was thoroughly ashamed of myself for having bothered him, although the few minutes of conversation were invaluable for the rest of my life.

Yet at the same time during his lectures he always seemed to recover. He might move to the rostrum with effort but after an hour and a half he walked away with the buoyancy of a young man. At these moments and during other times, he refreshed himself from the sources from which the spiritual vitality of the cosmos is maintained.

On the following night, 28th September, the eve of St. Michael's Day, Rudolf Steiner "raffte sich auf" and with super-human strength once more gathered all his energy together to give a lecture in honour of the festival of St. Michael. It had been a focusing point in his lectures during that summer to reveal the Archangel Michael as the Spirit of the Age, the inspiring and guiding Guardian of the present period of history. He had described him as the "fiery Prince of Thought" with whom the souls had been connected who are drawn into the Anthroposophical Movement and by whom they had been prepared and taught in a "Michael School" in the spirit-world before they descended into incarnation in this century.

The present "Last Address" is a transcript of what Rudolf Steiner said on that evening. It is a delicate, precious legacy. Technically it is a fragment. Rudolf Steiner requested that the transcript should not be made available before he had given the second half. But he was never able to complete the lecture. And thus it was eventually published as it stands, an earnest token, perhaps, of the fact that his very life—all too brief for his disciples and students in spite of the incredible wealth of his creative gifts—was cut short by the stone-walling of an uninspired, intellectually self-satisfied and basically dull age.

As it stands, the "Last Address" presents a serious problem of thought to Anthroposophists. Never before had Rudolf Steiner linked together the Individualities of John the Baptist and Lazarus-John in the manner in which he did it in this last lecture. Of the Individuality of John the Baptist he had spoken many times before. The spirit who lived in the Baptist was in fact treated by Rudolf Steiner as the paradigm of a representative sequence of consecutive lives of the same Individuality. Elijah—John the Baptist—Raphael—Novalis—this was the first series of reincarnations declared by Steiner early on in his teaching and never added to by any other examples until the very last months of his life. In their various ways these four historic personalities were the lives of the herald-angel of Christ.

The dramatic raising of Lazarus from the grave was an event which led to the elucidation of a different mystery. In his book, *Christianity as Mystical Fact*, published in 1902, Rudolf Steiner described this apparent "miracle" as an act of Initiation. In this act which represents a transitional form between the rituals of Initiation in the Mystery Temples of the ancient world and the dawning Christian era in which Initiations of this type are superseded altogether by inner developments, Lazarus became Lazarus-John, "the disciple whom Jesus loved" and the author of the Fourth Gospel. Although Rudolf Steiner spoke in the years after 1902 of this event, and of the figure who passed through it, many times and from many different sides, he never referred to another incarnation of Lazarus except on an intimate occasion, the content of which became known somewhat more generally only much later, after his death. But as already stated, he never connected John the Baptist and Lazarus-John in the manner suggested in the "Last

162

Address", and a previous incarnation of Lazarus which he indicated on the occasion mentioned above would seem to point in a different direction. Thus we are really left with a mystery.

Fortunately, some light has been thrown on this through a reply which Rudolf Steiner is reported to have given to a question of Dr. Ludwig Noll, the physician who together with Dr. Ita Wegman, the head of the Medical Section of the Goetheanum, attended him during his illness. We quote the postscript printed in the most recent German edition of the "Last Address".

"According to authenticated statements, the following verbal explanation was given by Rudolf Steiner to his physician, Dr. Ludwig Noll, in connection with the 'Last Address'.

"At the awakening of Lazarus, the spiritual Being, John the Baptist, who since his death had been the overshadowing Spirit of the disciples, penetrated from above into Lazarus as far as the Consciousness Soul; the Being of Lazarus himself, from below, intermingled with the spiritual Being of John the Baptist from above. After the awakening of Lazarus, this Being is Lazarus-John, the disciple whom the Lord loved."

This is a great help. But the present writer feels that even this illuminating comment still leaves some profound problems unanswered, and other readers and students of the "Last Address" may well share this feeling. The real core of the mystery seems to lie in the question: Did the two Individualities, the Baptist and the disciple whom Jesus loved, share their future incarnations? And if so, in what form?

Perhaps this is where we must leave the matter. In some other context Rudolf Steiner remarked with quiet seriousness that it is in certain respects better and more fruitful for the development of a human soul on its path to the spirit, if the soul has to ponder a spiritual problem rather than be furnished with a plain and neat answer. Did Rudolf Steiner leave the esoteric riddle of the "Last Address" with us, so that we might grow by pondering it reverently and thus be led eventually to revelations which we should find ourselves?

ALFRED HEIDENREICH

Lecture 11, "The Last Address"

My dear friends,

It has not been possible for me to speak to you on the last two days. But to-day—the day when the Michael mood of dedication must pour its light into all our heart and souls in readiness for the morrow—this day, my dear friends, I did not want to let pass without speaking to you at least a few words. That I am able to do so is due entirely to the loving and devoted care of our friend Dr. Ita Wegman. And so I hope that I will still be able to say to-day what I desire particularly to say to you on the occasion of this festival.

In recent months we have frequently spoken, my dear friends, of the instreaming of the Michael-Power into the spiritual events of man's life on earth. And it will be one of the more beautiful results that can follow from our anthroposophical understanding of times and seasons, if we are really able to add to the other festivals of the year a rightly ordered Michael Festival. That however will only be possible when the might and power of the Michael Thought, of which to-day men have no more than a dim feeling, has taken hold in a number of human souls who will then be able to create the right human starting-point for such a festival.

What we can do at present is to awaken, in this Michael time, the Michael mood in our souls by giving ourselves up to thoughts that will prepare the way for a future Michael Festival. And such thoughts are especially stirred to activity within us when we turn our gaze upon all that we have seen taking place—partly on Earth, partly in supersensible worlds—through long periods of time, in preparation for all that can now be accomplished for human evolution in the course of this present century by souls who in full sincerity feel themselves drawn to the Michael stream.

That you yourselves, my dear friends, in so far as you

truly and honestly incline to the Anthroposophical Movement, belong to these souls—this I have endeavoured to make clear to you in the lectures of the last weeks and especially also in the lectures where I spoke to you directly of the karma of the Anthroposophical Society. We can however carry these considerations a little further, and that is what I want to do to-day.

Let us now bring before our souls beings who are intimately connected, and will always be intimately connected, with the Michael stream, in the sense in which we have described it here. Let us direct our gaze to beings who in at least two successive incarnations made a powerful impression on great numbers of their fellow-men, beings who, however, only show themselves in their true unity when we recognise them as successive incarnations of one and the same being.

When we look back into olden times, we see rise up before us within the traditions of Judaism the prophetic figure of Elijah. We know what significance the prophet Elijah had for the people of the Old Testament, and therewith for all mankind; we know how he set before them the goal and destiny of their existence. And we have shown how in the course of time the being who was present in Elijah appeared again at the very most important moment of human evolution, appeared again so that Christ Jesus Himself could give him the Initiation he was to receive for the evolution of mankind. For the being of Elijah appeared again in Lazarus-John—who are in truth one and the same figure, as you will have understood from my book *Christianity as Mystical Fact*.

And further we saw that this being appears once more in that world painter who let his artistic power unfold in marvellous depths of tenderness, as it moved hovering over the Mystery of Golgotha. And we saw how the deeply Christian impulse that lived in Raphael, as it were impelling into colour and form the very nature and being of Christianity itself—we saw how this impulse rose again in the poet Novalis. In the poet Novalis stands revealed in wondrously beautiful words what Raphael had placed before mankind in colours and forms of rarest loveliness. We see, thus following one another in time, beings who are brought together into a unity when incarnation is understood.

We know (for I have often spoken with you of these things) how, when man has gone through the gate of death, he enters the world of stars. What we are accustomed to call "stars" in the external, physical sense are no more than the outer sign and symbol of spiritual worlds which look down upon us and take their share and part in all the deeds of the evolution of mankind.

We know that man passes through the Moon sphere and through the spheres of Mercury and Venus, through the spheres of the Sun and of Mars, and of Jupiter and Saturn. And we know that when, together with the beings of these spheres and together too with other human souls who have also departed from the life on Earth, he has elaborated his karma, he then turns back again to earthly existence.

Bearing this in mind, let us look for a moment at Raphael and see how he passes through the gate of death, and how he enters the realm of the starry worlds, the realm of spiritual evolution, taking with him the power of his art, which already on Earth shone with the bright light of the stars. We behold, my dear friends, how Raphael enters the Moon sphere, and we see how he comes into association here with the Spirits who live in the Moon sphere and who are the spiritual Individualities of the great original Leaders of mankind, with whose wisdom Raphael, as Elijah, had been deeply inspired. He meets these Moon Beings, and he meets too all the souls with whom he has lived in earlier stages of Earth-evolution. We see how he unites himself spiritually with the spiritual origin of the Earth, with that World of Being which first made it possible for man to be, and for the Earthly to be impregnated with the Divine. We behold Raphael as it were completely "at home", united with those with whom he had most loved to be in the Elijah existence, inasmuch as it was They who at the beginning of Earth existence set the goal for the life of this Earth.

Then we behold him wandering through the Mercury sphere where, in association with the great Cosmic Healers, he transforms for his spirituality the power that had been his to create what is so infinitely whole and healthy in colour and line. All that he has painted, whether on canvas or as a fresco on the wall, for the help and comfort as well as for the unending inspiration of such as can understand—all his work that was so radiant with light, showed itself now to him in the great cosmic connection in which it is able to stand when it passes through the Beings of the Mercury sphere.

And thus was he, who on Earth had unfolded so great a love for art, whose soul had been aflame with love for colour and for line, transplanted now into the sphere of Venus, which in turn lovingly bore him across to the Sun, to that Sun existence which lived in all his incarnations so far as they are yet known to us. For it was from the *Sun* that he, as the prophet Elijah, brought to mankind through the medium of his own people the truths that belong to the goals of existence.

We see how in the Sun sphere he is able to live through over again in a deep and intimate sense—in another way now than when he was on Earth as a companion of Christ Jesus—he is able to live over again what he underwent when, through the Initiation of Christ Jesus, he, Lazarus, became John.

And all that he has painted in shining light for the followers of Christ Jesus—he now beholds all this pour its rays into the cosmic transformation of the human heart.

And we see further how what he thus had at the foundation of his life penetrates, wisdom-filled, the sphere of Jupiter. In this sphere he is able in wisdom to enter into a relation of understanding with such spirits as Goethe—the spirit, that is, that afterwards became Goethe—as well as also with spirits who had gone astray on other paths, but who nevertheless led over World Being and World Thought into the realm of the magical. The foundation is laid for his magic idealism in the experience he had of the evolution of

168

the later Eliphas Levi. And we behold too how he partakes in all that was living there in Swedenborg.

And now I must draw your attention to something in the life of Raphael that is of very great significance. A personality who was most deeply devoted to Raphael—Hermann Grimm—set to work four times to write a life of Raphael. His *Life of Michelangelo* he brought to a beautiful completeness, but he never succeeded in drawing any picture of Raphael's earthly life that gave him satisfaction. In his own view all he wrote was unfinished and incomplete. The first book he undertook was intended to be a biography. What is it? Nothing but a reproduction of old anecdotes told by Vasari! No biography of Raphael at all, but something altogether different—a description of what Raphael became on Earth after his death, in the respect and recognition of his fellow men. Hermann Grimm relates what people have thought of Raphael—what the Italians, the French, the Germans have thought of Raphael in the course of history through the centuries. What he gives us is a biography of the Raphael Thought as it has lived here on Earth since his death. He finds the way to tell what remains of Raphael in the hearts and minds of men, what lives of him still in their reverence and understanding. But he does not find the possibility to give a picture of the earthly life of Raphael.

After Hermann Grimm has made the attempt four times over, he says: All that one can really do for Raphael as a personality is to write of how one picture passes over into the next, as though it had been painted by a supersensible being who had simply not touched the Earth at all with his earthly life. The *pictures* are there, and one can look right away from Raphael who painted the pictures and reproduce the sequence of what is expressed in their inner content.

And so, shortly before his death, Hermann Grimm began to speak once again about Raphael; yet once more he made the attempt to put pen to paper and write about him. This time however he spoke only of his pictures and not about the earthly personality of Raphael at all.

The truth is, my dear friends, this earthly personality of Raphael was completely yielded up and was only present through what Lazarus-John gave to this soul to be poured out into colour and line for all mankind.

Such was the life of this being. And it was so, that this Raphael life could only be, as it were, absolved in *another* life of thirty years—in Novalis. And so we see Raphael die young, Novalis die young—*one being*, who came forth from Elijah-John, appearing before mankind in two different forms, preparing through art and through poetry the true Michael mood of soul, sent down by the Michael stream as messenger to men on Earth.

And now we behold the wonderful artistic power of Raphael come to life again in Novalis in *poetry* that stirs and enraptures the hearts of men. All that through Raphael was given to human eyes to see—of this could human hearts drink deep, when it came again in Novalis.

When we consider the life of Novalis, what an echo we find there of the Raphael life for which Hermann Grimm had so fine an understanding! His beloved dies in her youth. He is himself still young. What is he going to do with his life now that she has died? He tells us himself. He says that his life on Earth will be henceforth to "die after her", to follow her on the way of death. He wants to pass over already now into the supersensible, to lead again the Raphael life, not touching the Earth, but living out in poetry his magic idealism. He would fain not let himself be touched by Earth life.

When we read the *Fragments* of Novalis, and give ourselves up to the life that flows so abundantly in them, we can discover the secret of the deep impression they make on us. Whatever we have before us in immediate sense-reality, whatever the eye can see and recognise as beautiful—all this, through the magic idealism that lives in the soul of Novalis, appears in his poetry with a well-nigh heavenly splendour. The meanest and simplest material thing—with the magic idealism of his poetry he can make it live again in all its spiritual light and glory.

And so we see in Novalis a radiant and splendid fore-runner of that Michael stream which is now to lead you all, my dear friends, while you live; and then, after you have gone through the gate of death, you will find in the spiritual supersensible worlds all those others—among them also the being of whom I have been speaking to you to-day—all those with whom you are to prepare the work that shall be accomplished at the end of the century, and that shall lead mankind past the great crisis in which it is involved.

This work is: to let the Michael Power and the Michael Will penetrate the whole of life. The Michael Power and the Michael Will are none other than the Christ Will and the Christ Power, going before in order to implant in the right way into the Earth the Power of the Christ. If this Michael Power is able verily to overcome all that is of the demon and the dragon (and you well know what that is), if you all, who have in this way received in the light the Michael Thought, have indeed received it with true and faithful heart and with tender love, and will endeavour to go forward from the Michael mood of this year, until not only is the Michael Thought *revealed* in your soul, but you are able also to make the Michael Thought *live* in your *deeds* in all its strength and all its power—if this is so, then will you be true servants of the Michael Thought, worthy helpers of what has now to enter Earth-evolution through Anthroposophy, and take its place there in the meaning of Michael.

If, in the near future, in four times twelve human beings, the Michael Thought becomes fully alive—four times twelve human beings, that is, who are recognised not by themselves but by the Leadership of the Goetheanum in Dornach—if in four times twelve such human beings, leaders arise having the mood of soul that belongs to the Michael festival, then we can look up to the light that through the Michael stream and the Michael activity will be shed abroad in the future among mankind.

Because this is so, my dear friends, I have made the effort to-day to rise up and speak to you, if only in these few short words. My strength is not sufficient for more to-day. May

171

the words so speak to your soul that you receive the Michael Thought in the sense of what a faithful follower of Michael may feel when, clothed in the light rays of the Sun, Michael appears and points us to that which must now take place. For it must even be so that this Michael garment, this garment of Light, shall become the Words of the Worlds, which are the Christ Words—the Words of the Worlds, which can transform the Logos of the Worlds into the Logos of Mankind. Therefore let my words to you to-day be these:

> Springing from Powers of the Sun,
> Radiant Spirit-powers, blessing all Worlds!
> For Michael's garment of rays
> Ye are predestined by Thought Divine.

> He, the Christ-messenger, revealeth in you—
> Bearing mankind aloft—the sacred Will of Worlds.
> Ye, the radiant Beings of Aether-Worlds,
> Bear the Christ-Word to Man.

> Thus shall the Herald of Christ appear
> To the thirstily waiting souls,
> To whom your Word of Light shines forth
> In cosmic age of Spirit-Man.

> Ye, the disciples of Spirit-Knowledge,
> Take Michael's Wisdom beckoning,
> Take the Word of Love of the Will of Worlds
> Into your soul's aspiring, actively!

Publisher's Note Regarding Rudolf Steiner's Lectures

The lectures contained in this volume have been translated from the German which is based on stenographic and other recorded texts that were in most cases never seen or revised by the lecturer. Hence, due to human errors in hearing and transcription, they may contain mistakes and faulty passages. Every effort has been made to ensure that this is not the case. Some of the lectures were given to audiences more familiar with anthroposophy; these are the so-called 'private' or 'members' lectures. Other lectures, like the written works, were intended for the general public. The differences between these, as Rudolf Steiner indicates in his *Autobiography*, is twofold. On the one hand, the members' lectures take for granted a background in and commitment to anthroposophy; in the public lectures this was not the case. At the same time, the members' lectures address the concerns and dilemmas of the members, while the public work speaks directly out of Steiner's own understanding of universal needs. Nevertheless, as Rudolf Steiner stresses: 'Nothing was ever said that was not solely the result of my direct experience of the growing content of anthroposophy. There was never any question of concessions to the prejudices and preferences of the members. Whoever reads these privately printed lectures can take them to represent anthroposophy in the fullest sense. Thus it was possible without hesitation—when the complaints in this direction became too persistent—to depart from the custom of circulating this material "for members only". But it must be borne in mind that faulty passages do occur in these reports not revised by myself.' Earlier in the same chapter, he states: 'Had I been able to correct them [the private lectures] the restriction [for members only] would have been unnecessary from the beginning.'